PROFITABLE
PRACTICE

WHY A DENTAL PRACTICE
IS AN EXCEPTIONAL INVESTMENT

Timothy A. Brown

Copyright © Timothy Brown,
2009, 2012, 2014, 2015, 2017

Published by ECW Press
665 Gerrard Street East
Toronto, Ontario M4M 1Y2

Printing: Friesens 10 9 8 7

PRINTED AND BOUND IN CANADA

LIBRARY AND ARCHIVES CANADA
CATALOGUING IN PUBLICATION

Brown, Timothy A
Profitable practice: why a dental
practice is an exceptional investment
/ Timothy A. Brown.

Includes bibliographical references.
ISBN-13: 978-1-55022-850-2
ISBN-10: 1-55022-850-1

1. Dental offices—Canada—
Management. 1. Title.

RK58.7.C3B76 2009   651'.961760971
C2009-900947-1

Cover and text design: Tania Craan
Cover image © Koksharov Dmitry

"The physician should know what the physician before him has known, if he does not want to defraud himself and others."
— HIPPOCRATES

This book is dedicated to my father, Roy Brown. Thanks to his vision and determination, countless dentists have sold their practices and retired with dignity and profitably.

Table of Contents

"You don't write because you want to say something;
you write because you've got something to say."
— F. SCOTT FITZGERALD

My career has been a product of my father's life
work. This book is meant to honour him and my
mother, Joan, who supported him and helped him
build his company. With *Profitable Practice* I also hope
to continue his goal of allowing dentists "to retire
with dignity."

I wish to thank the following dentists for their
inspiration over the last twenty years: Dr. Howard
Rocket, Dr. Jerry Isenberg, Dr. John Wilson, Dr.
John Badger, Dr. Jeff Williams, Dr. Wayne Raborn,
Dr. Marcia Boyd, Dr. Dev Mangat, Ann Wright, Tom
Schramm, Bill Alton, and especially my dear friend
Dr. Roger Ellis.

As well, with thanks to Dr. Bruce Glazer, who gra-
ciously gave me a copy of the greatest text I have
ever read about dental practice management, written
by George Wood Clapp, D.D.S., in 1916 and entitled
Profitable Practice.

I am indebted to G. Christen and Peter M. Pronych
for documenting the great history of Painless Parker.
Many references to Parker's fascinating history are
contained in this book.

I am deeply grateful for the aid and ideas provided

by my sisters, Lanee Brown and Sally Brown, my patient wife, Sandy Evans, and my very good friend and editor, Jim Ruddy. Lastly, thanks to my nephews Robert MacDonald and David Rourke, who aspire to follow in their grandfather's footsteps.

The majority of the text to follow is a collection of wisdom and stories given by dentists in the course of the research of this book. In essence, it constitutes dentists giving advice to other dentists. The advice was offered freely and candidly in order to alert other dentists to some of the pitfalls of a dental practice. In short, these dentists wanted others to benefit from their experiences and mistakes.

Also, this book is intended to be a guideline to recent dental graduates. ROI Corporation wishes you great success. In addition, veteran dentists well into the middle stages of their career will find many good suggestions and best practices that may be of assistance, or at least confirm what they already know. Lastly, dentists in the final stages of their career will find sound advice on how to sell their practice and retire with dignity.

"Those Were the Days"

In the 1950s, when I met with dentists who had just graduated, their primary concern was what location to select to start a new practice. The major consideration was: do you want to set up an office near to where you want to live or to set up where you are needed? Since new patient flow was more than adequate almost everywhere, most dentists chose to go to where they wanted to live. The established dentists of Canada were booked solid for many months in advance. Most enjoyed a relaxed workweek of nine to five, taking either Wednesday or Friday off, and rarely did a dentist work an evening or a weekend.

Sixty years ago more than 90% of dental school graduates were male. Since there were few plazas, shopping centres or medical dental offices, they looked for offices on the second floor above an existing store.

The ideal set-up was a corner office with windows on both corners and room on the wall for advertising their practice. Some landlords were hesitant to lease or rent to a dentist, as they were concerned about the potential plumbing problems that might occur and the damage that would result to the tenants below. However, dentists became prized tenants for two reasons: they were prompt with their rent payments, and they usually stayed twenty or more years in the same location. Still, the leaseholds were expensive as they needed small partitioned rooms with specialized plumbing and wiring. These specialized rooms proved challenging and costly. Landlords provided many of the required improvements and charged two to five dollars per square foot for prime locations.

The cost of opening a new office ranged from $7,000 to $10,000. A single operatory with new equipment cost about $5,000. This included a chair, delivery unit, x-ray, lights, cabinet, sterilization, compressor, lathe and darkroom tank. There weren't any Cavitrons, high-speed handpieces, pan x-rays or computers to be purchased. When the dentist's office was finished, he or she was usually fully booked within the first week of operation.

Staffing was without chair-side assistants or hygienists. The doctor required one receptionist/nurse who booked patients, collected fees, cleaned up and, if time allowed, would mix materials. The patient sat upright with an articulating head and footrest (like a barber's chair). The dentist stood up. The delivery unit was also an upright, floor-mounted device with an engine, a chair, two syringes (water and air), a cuspidor and a saliva injector. That's all.

Steel burrs were sold by the half gross; there were no carbide burrs or slow speed engines with belts and handpieces with speeds of 2000–5000 rpm. Dentists applied pressure as there were no lubricants or cooling when cutting was needed. Replacement of fillings was common because materials for anterior silicates and amalgam silicates or porcelains often washed out.

Fees were low. A filling cost from $5 to $9; an extraction was $5 to $10; dentures started at about $85; x-rays cost about $3 each. There was little or no endodontics, cosmetic surgery or implants.

A good day's gross was $400 to $500 resulting in an income of $80,000 to $100,000 per year with over-head of 40%. The size of most offices ranged between 500 and 750 square feet, with two operatories (one that was empty and unused for varying lengths of time), a small lab, a darkroom, both a business office and pri-vate office and a waiting room. Many dentists resisted equipping the second operatory because they could only treat one patient at a time. Eventually, it became efficient and profitable to have a nurse who could clean up one operatory and set up a patient in the other.

Practices were rarely bought or sold. Most practices simply closed due to retirement or health concerns. The location might merit the sale price of $5,000 for the used equipment and the traditional payment for goodwill was $1, only to make it legal!

In the late 1950s many changes slowly occurred and then accelerated dramatically through the 1960s and

1970s. These changes included chair-side assistants and technical advances such as high-speed air turbines and wash field cooling spray vacuums. Time and motion and quadrant dentistry came into practice. Denturists and hygienists did much of the cleaning and mundane duties of the practice, leaving dentists to concentrate on the technical and complicated aspects. At the same time, dental insurance plans paid for more treatments than before.

Today, more than 60 years later, the result of those changes and many others is staggering. A brand new dental office is usually 1,500 to 2,000 square feet, with four to six operatories, and built with superior equipment for associates and hygienists. Average annual gross income now ranges from $750,000 to over $1 million. The key to a successful new practice is constant new patient flow — and the competition for new patients is fierce!

Most dentists are being advised to buy an established practice by their bankers and accountants if only to benefit from immediate cash flow. This ensures steady, daily patient flow from the first day and avoids many of the pitfalls of high set-up costs and rents. The typical established practice now sells for over $1 million dollars.

Ah, to think back to the 1950s — those were the days . . .

ROY BROWN

Roy Brown is the Chairman Emeritus of ROI Corporation, Canada's largest dental practice appraiser and broker.

DENTISTRY AS A BUSINESS

CHAPTER 1

The History of Dental Practice Management

• •

When Did the First Practice Manager Offer Advice to a Dentist?

There are no industry records that show practice management was ever seen as a necessary course of study in any schools of dentistry, nor was it valued as a criterion of a successful practice. The first advice given to a dentist was likely from a spouse or a banker, hardly experts in dental practice management. Once in practice, dentists would typically look to their colleagues for tips on how to build a practice. This process did not guarantee success.

Who Then Pioneered the Modern Practice Management Industry?

Dr. George Wood Clapp's book entitled *Profitable Practice*, written in 1916, offered the following advice:

> *"Dentistry as means of service is a profession; as a means of livelihood it is a business."*

Further, in his opening remarks, Clapp thanked those who gave him guidance:

> *"May their efforts speed the day when the discussion of the business elements in practice will receive the same full, free and beneficial discussion that is now accorded to technical questions. Then will dawn the day of fees that are fair to patients and to dentists."*

Clearly, these are wise words that foresee the need for professional advice.

Definition of Practice Management

While there is no one industry definition that is acceptable to all, the following provides a working statement for the purposes of this book:

> *"The art and science of running a profitable dental practice."*

Painless Parker (a.k.a. Edgar Randolph), a man famous for pioneering the advertising of dental services to America in the early 1900s, has his definition:

> *"You have to be organized, systematized, capitalized, advertised, standardized, and specialized. These are the major principles of business economics."*

Painless Parker idolized P.T. Barnum, the owner of the

world's greatest circus. Barnum offered this advice to Painless:

> *"The great secret of anything is to get a hearing. Half the object is gained when the audience is assembled."*

Arthur Schopenhauer, the famous German philosopher of the nineteenth century, wrote:

> *"If you want to achieve something in business, in writing, in painting, you must follow the rules without knowing them."*

These words ring true today. Practice management is not any different now than it was in the early years of dentistry.

The four simple steps to successful practice management are:

1. Greet the patient.
2. Treat the patient.
3. Bill and collect fees.
4. Remind them to return and repeat the process.

Advertising is an essential promotional tool to expand a dental practice. Treating the patient effectively is the sole responsibility of the dentist. Billing and collecting, and then reminding them to return for continuing treatments (recall programs), are the responsibilities of all the staff in the modern dental practice.

Who Then Is the Practice Manager?

Some dentists do employ office managers to perform the majority of day-to-day routine requirements, but ultimately it is the dentist, as owner of the practice, who is the official practice manager. He/she must decide on the key elements of how to position the practice in the marketplace, given the many variables that Painless Parker mentions:

1. *Organization* — This involves the selection of financial record-keeping systems, charting systems and recall systems.
2. *Systemization* — This mandates integrating the above organizational tools into a highly repetitive and accurate process.
3. *Capitalization* — This requires securing financial resources from personal, family or financial institutions to adequately equip the practice with the tools of the trade necessary to deliver service in a timely and profitable fashion.
4. *Advertising* — This requires promoting your service to the public and attracting people to your unique offering as opposed to other dental practices.
5. *Standardization* — This necessitates perfecting the delivery systems in all regards so that the final results are consistent with the intended service level offering.
6. *Specialization* — This involves mastering the dental service and offering that service at the highest level possible. It also involves recognizing when a dental practice cannot meet the needs of the patient and recommending a dental practice that can.

CHAPTER 2

The History of ROI Corporation

• •

The author's father, Roy Brown, began selling dental supplies in 1948, at the age of 18. He joined the Associated Dentists Cooperative (ADC) as a junior salesman and was assigned a territory based out of London, Ontario. The ADC was owned and managed by a revolving board of directors that consisted almost exclusively of dentists.

The ADC was founded in response to an investigation by the Canadian Department of Justice to determine if an alleged combine in the manufacture and sale of dental supplies existed within Canada. The July 28, 1947, report, submitted by the Right Honourable J.L. Ilsley K.C., Minister of Justice, concluded the following:

"A combine exists in the distribution and sale of dental supplies in Canada."

The ADC was formed because a group of entrepreneurial dentists decided to take the purchase and distribution of dental supplies into their own hands. The ADC was a for-profit cooperative that redistributed dividends to the shareholders — most of whom were dentists who purchased their goods from the company.

During Roy Brown's 26-year career with the ADC, he pioneered many services of the profession. The ADC owned the first equipment-leasing company. He was successful in bringing Siemens dental equipment (now Sirona) to Canada. Many dentists will recognize the famous 50 KV x-ray units that are still in use today, almost 40 years later!

As Roy worked his way up to general manager and then president, he became aware that many of the board member dentists were aging and retirement was nearing.

Who would take over their established practices?

After a lengthy career with the ADC, later named Healthco in the early 1970s, Roy Brown wanted to assist dentists to leave their practices with dignity and a profit — thus he formed ROI Management (later renamed ROI Corporation) in 1974.

At first dentists were skeptical. Until then, when dentists retired they simply closed the doors, stored the equipment, terminated staff and advised patients to seek treatment elsewhere. There were very few "transitions" from one dentist to another, and rarely was a practice actually sold.

In 1974, Roy met with one of the most established and successful dentists in Toronto. This dentist was frustrated at the prospect of shutting down his very well-equipped and successful practice. He commissioned Roy to act as his agent and to find him a replacement dentist to take over. He set his asking price at $28,000.

Later that year, Roy identified a suitable dentist, a contract was negotiated, and what appears to be the very first "brokered" sale of a dental practice was documented in Canada. The price paid? Exactly $28,000!

CHAPTER 3

The Dentist as Business Person

• • • • • • • • • • • • • • • • • • • •

"I'm not a good business person."

Sadly, this is a common statement made by dentists. This belief is largely untrue and only perpetuates the myth of business incompetence with regard to dentists.

There are many clever and well-trained individuals who sell to the dental profession. Most are reputable persons who are partnered with the profession for mutual success. Others are less than reputable and find that dentists are often easy prey for their gimmicks and wares.

"Truth carried to an extreme may become an untruth, and some of the speakers and writers who have grown up with the pale of the code have taken some principles

to nonsensical extremes which have been very harmful to dentists who have been misled thereby."
— GEORGE WOOD CLAPP

"Making the simple complicated is commonplace: making the complicated simple, awesomely simple — that's creativity."
— CHARLES MINGUS

Why Do Dentists Believe They Are Not Good Business People?

The notion starts in university and then is perpetuated by the dentists themselves and their advisors. Dentists often enter dental school with ideals and dreams of what dentistry will be like. They have visions of running a small business, having loyal staff and patients who adore them, working with their hands and earning an above average income.

The economics of a dental practice are largely ignored and the science of dentistry becomes the entire focus of the curriculum. The business of dentistry is rarely discussed at this formative stage and service to patients dominates the teaching of dental students.

This is, perhaps, as it should be.

When Should Dental Economics Be Taught to Dental Students?

Research interviews with hundreds of dentists reveal that they never received instruction in sound business practices. Virtually all the dentists who graduated from the 1950s to the early 2000s state that they were inadequately prepared and lacked confidence in their ability to run a dental practice.

The purchase of an established practice has become fashionable, partly due to the fact that the business has been up and running for many years. Thus the formation of the business model is much less of a challenge to the dentist who buys a practice.

> *"The young dentist without commercial experience who can get a position in an office where good business and professional methods are practised is usually much better off, in the end, than he who starts out 'on his own.'"*
> — GEORGE WOOD CLAPP

While Clapp had many opinions on how to establish a dental practice, his advice to find a position in an existing office was, and still is, the best advice that a young graduate can follow.

Why try to learn all the secrets of successful practice when hundreds of thousands have done it before you?

Dental schools train dentists to be competent. Working within a practice as an associate dentist will expose young dentists to the simplicity of the business model, after which they are prepared to confidently take over their own practice.

Advisors to the profession come in many forms and have varying degrees of knowledge and competency. However, the art and science of running a successful practice is best learned while on the job and from those who actually own a practice. Dental advisors profit from a dentist's need for their counsel, and some may even suggest that young dentists hand over this critical aspect of their business to them as they offer to take care of the business while the dentists focus on the dentistry.

In the end this becomes a foolhardy practice as ultimately dentists alone are responsible for their practices. Certainly advisors should provide counsel on legal and financial matters such as the unknown aspects of taxation, but they should not become the official practice manager.

Many dentists who completely hand over the role of practice manager to third parties invariably regret having done so. One such dentist, who graduated in 1946, exemplifies what many other dentists have said:

"The patients are the practice, all the rest is just paperwork!"
— I. LIGHTMAN, D.D.S

Who Is Qualified to Offer Practice Management Advice?

Most advisors, including the author, have never worked a single day in a dental office — therefore, how can such advisors possibly understand what it's really like?

While this is true, reputable advisors have spent countless hours in many dental offices observing both good and bad practices. These advisors gather data and insight from across Canada. The best advisors are aware of new developments and technical advances. These people are in the business of assessing successful dental and business practices in order to adequately evaluate what such practices are financially worth.

New dentists often underestimate their ability to start a new practice in a new area or location. They often put their trust in others to help them, sometimes with disastrous results.

Dentists are trained to measure precisely their clinical work. They work in small rooms, with small instruments, in a very small space (the mouth) and apply their skills in very small hand movements.

Practice management, on the other hand, requires broad vision and macroeconomic thinking. When the details of practice management are addressed and issues that require a wider perspective arise, dentists can become fixated on the minutiae and often overanalyze or dissect practice management issues to the extreme.

Running an exceptional practice is more than science; it is very much an art. It requires great people skills for dealing with staff and patients. Patients must perceive that the office is well run by qualified and caring individuals. They must have a sense of trust and confidence. Staff members must be made to feel a part of a team that respects each other and has a common goal of providing first-rate dental care. Staff members have to be encouraged and coached regularly to genuinely take pride in what they are doing and in communicating their concern for their patients. The working environment must be pleasing and amicable for all this to happen.

Dentists are much better trained to be scientists than artists. This is why they have such a large need for practice management training in dental school, and because it is lacking, this is also why dentists seek the help of "experts" to assist them. Perhaps this book can help to reduce the need for costly and often controversial practice managers.

CHAPTER 4

The Dental Consumer

. . . .

Will There Be Adequate Demand for the Dental Services in the Future?

In the 1960s some predicted dire consequences for dentists with the introduction of fluoride in the water treatment system. Some dentists even predicted their own demise.

Today, dentistry is thriving! Canadians spend at least $15 billion a year on dental care. In part, this is due to improved technology allowing new and better procedures. As well, public education has instilled a need for greater dental care. Lastly, there has been a much greater demand in the highly lucrative area of cosmetic dentistry.

The primary dental consumer (the patient) is the baby boomer. Typically, this person is about fifty years of age and will have a huge impact on the dental practices for at least another twenty years! These men and women are entering their prime personal care spending years.

Research suggests that the total annual spending on dental care will exceed $20 billion before the year 2020. This will be largely a result of the baby boomers' desire to look better and their willingness to spend on themselves.

Unlike previous generations, boomers see dental cosmetics as an entitlement and an investment in themselves. Many patients are seeking instant gratification in this regard. This raises many ethical issues for some dentists.

Should they do procedures that would remove or alter perfectly good teeth simply for the sake of good looks? Should they deprive themselves of the lucrative fees they could charge for such treatments? Should they deny their patients' demands for dental cosmetics? Research indicates that it is unlikely that the demand for cosmetic procedures will diminish any time soon.

Where Are Dental Services in the Greatest Demand?

The leading indicator of demand for dental services is the ratio of dentists to the total population. Today, ratios range from 1:1,000 in the major cities to in excess of 1:2,500 in rural and remote Canada.

Unfortunately, most methods of calculating ratios are unreliable. They purely "count" the number of dentists registered to practice in a given parameter — usually a city or town. This number is then divided by the published population figures. This ignores several key factors:

- The actual equivalent full-time ratio of dentists (how many work a full-time schedule in that given area)
- The propensity of those dentists to continue in full-time practice for an unknown duration.

A few years back, a charming young dentist indicated that she would not move to a particular community because she had determined that there were too many dentists in the town already. When asked what her method was for determining this, she carefully explained that she had examined the telephone directory and the dental college listing of dentists. She then divided the number of names into the town's population figure (as provided by the town on their welcome sign while entering the community). She concluded that there was one dentist for every 1,500 people. This ratio was lower than the 1:2,000 ratio her professors had suggested was necessary to start a practice.

By chance, the author happened to know all the dentists in that town, their ages, and their work schedules. With this data, a calculation of the actual equivalent full-time dentists was made. A visit to the local government website revealed the current population was actually higher. The population sign had not been updated in years. With the corrected numbers, the actual ratio was 1:2,200 — almost 40% better than the young dentist had concluded.

Thus, when seeking a dental practice opportunity in any area, using names and population figures may not yield an accurate ratio. Research suggests a deduction of 15% to 25% should be made from the names in the various directories for part-time and semi- or fully-retired dentists. Their names still appear even though they have retired or greatly reduced their workload.

Until the 1970s there was a limited but adequate supply of equivalent full-time (EFT) dentists in most regions. Then, for two decades, the dental schools increased class sizes, increasing the supply of dentists faster than the growth in population. Thus the number of dentists increased, mostly in the major cities.

A profile of recent graduates reveals that the female majority (over 60%) show a preference for living in large cities, and if gender is removed, we see large majorities of new dentists are from cultures that prefer to stay in the larger cities for family and community reasons. This shift in the demographics of the graduating classes for the next decade will continue to have a serious impact upon ratios in the major cities.

For the foreseeable future, dentists will continue to choose to live and work in urban and suburban areas, thus limiting the EFT supply in rural and remote regions. This trend will continue to impact the sale prices of practices everywhere. Major city practices will remain valuable, while those practices situated in remote rural areas will likely decline in value.

In conclusion, overall demand for dental services will increase due to the needs of an aging population and the trend toward cosmetic dentistry. Consequently, dental practices are, and will remain, a very good investment in the major Canadian cities and suburbs for the foreseeable future.

Career Models

CHAPTER 5

The New Graduate Dentist and the Associate Experience

• •

The long process of becoming a qualified dentist is over. Now what? Some dentists will go directly into postgraduate studies or internships. Others take a long-deserved vacation, but most will go into practice as an associate.

Associating has many advantages:

• *No additional financial burden* — The principal pays all the bills and invests in the facility and equipment; thus the new graduate has the opportunity to pay off student debts or to save for future needs.
• *Little management responsibility* — The principal is the practice manager; thus the associate is able to focus on building clinical competency and patient management skills.
• *Freedom to move on short notice and to pursue*

other opportunities — Most principals ask for one or two months notice; unfortunately, many associates leave on very short notice. This practice is not recommended as it invariably creates hard feelings and potential future repercussions.

The disadvantages are:

- *Lack of authority for major decision making* — The principal controls the new graduate's schedule and patient flow — sometimes to the point where he/she is working at a much slower pace than desired.
- *A slowly increasing income curve* — It takes a year or two to earn the trust of the principal, staff and patients before the associate is working at the pace required to earn what is necessary for rapid debt reduction or savings.
- *Short notice terminations are common* when the associate and the principal have a different philosophy that leaves the associate out of work when he/she could be earning income.
- *Many associates work in multiple practices* as most principals can only offer two or three days of patient flow.

The alternatives are to set up a new office from scratch or to buy an established practice to eliminate these disadvantages. Historically, the new graduate is not ready for either of these commitments for at least three to five years. Thus, the associateship is the choice of the large majority, even with the obvious shortcomings.

The Associate Buy-In (a.k.a. "Hire the Buyer")

Some associate positions are undertaken with the intent to buy into the practice at a later date. Some associate agreements have the time and price more or less agreed upon at the outset. Unfortunately, these intentions are often postponed or abandoned as the relationship between principal and associate develops. Like many marriages, the intentions are for a long-term commitment, but often this is not the case. People and professionals may grow apart in their plans and dreams and many agreements are broken off prematurely.

Principals are advised to avoid any promise of ownership when hiring an associate dentist. Principals often use the promise of ownership to attract a suitable associate. Usually, they expect the associate to work evenings, Fridays and weekends. They give the associate difficult patients and difficult procedures. A case in point involved a dentist who hired an associate for the above reasons. The associate demanded an ownership offering after one year. Reluctantly, the dentist conceded. However, after a short time, the arrangement made was unsatisfactory. The associate sued for a constructive dismissal and received a sizeable settlement.

Interviews with many young associates reveal they agree to a commitment to buy in because they want the position to gain experience and earn income. One unscrupulous associate admitted he had copied the computer records of the principal's practice and was planning to open an office nearby. He confessed that some of the staff were prepared to move with him and in effect a mutiny was in the making. Principals are advised to be wary and ascertain the true intentions of their associate.

Obviously both the principal and the associate should adhere to fair business practices. Many young graduates are not ready for an ownership agreement because of their personal circumstances. Some will marry and start families and may not want to stay in a particular area. Ownership demands a commitment and a sense of permanence.

Associates who choose to align with a principal are advised to seek an Associate Agreement. The agreement (see Appendix B for a sample copy) should not contain any mention of buying in or buying the practice outright. This would be premature for both parties. The Associate Agreement should be a contract focusing only on the employment conditions. Agreements to purchase should be negotiated at a later date, once compatibility has been determined and suitable timelines can be defined. This is typically a one or two year process.

Despite the importance of such agreements, research suggests that less than half of principal and associate relationships do not have a signed agreement in place. This is a recipe for disaster as either party could terminate the relationship at any time. This agreement should define many common practices. For example, associates typically feel entitled to contact the patients they have brought into the office, while principals often feel that such patients belong to the practice.

So who is correct? The regulatory colleges have strict guidelines as to how and when dentists can contact patients for commercial purposes, but they normally do not intervene in commercial disputes. Thus, when departing dentists begin the fight over patients, an expensive lawsuit often results. A written agreement may have prevented this wasteful and often humiliating struggle. ROI Corporation surveys show many dentists' friendships have been lost in this way.

CHAPTER 6

The Career Associate and the Locum Dentist

● ●

The Career Associate

There are many very successful associate arrangements whereby neither party wishes to be partners and the junior is happy to remain as an associate for life. Female dentists may seek this arrangement to allow them the opportunity to raise a family. Most wish to establish their own practice but often at a later time in their career.

Locum Dentists — An Emerging Career Choice

The presence of the temporary dentist (the "temp") in the workplace has become more and more commonplace. Often these dentists have sold their practices but still wish to continue to practice, on a reduced schedule. Typically, these dentists have registered with a locum service. A dentist may also "temp" for the person who has bought his/her practice, when the purchaser takes holidays or temporary leaves for maternity, medical or other reasons. This makes perfect sense as patients and staff are most accepting of the former, and familiar, dentist. Production is usually maintained at similar levels, thus keeping the practice vibrant while the principal is off.

Medical doctors have been practising as locums for decades. Many associates never plan or want to own their own practice. They come and go as required, and are content to do so. Many dentists are on the verge of adopting this career choice.

The benefits of being a locum, much like those of an associate, are:

- *No financial commitment.*
- *Intermittent work* — You might work one or two months, then have one or two months off.
- *No burden of management* — The principal makes the decisions.
- *Freedom* — Some mature locums have limited family commitments and welcome the freedom to travel, pursue hobbies or live an alternative lifestyle.

The primary benefit of hiring a locum dentist is the ability to take a leave. Maternity leaves, due to the proliferation of female dentists, are about to increase substantially. Who will cover for these expectant mothers? Locums are needed!

Baby boomer dentists (those born between 1946 and 1964) are the majority of today's practitioners, and they are the most likely to experience a disability. Hundreds of interviews with dentists who are selling their practices reveal a large majority are doing so because of a disability. The locum is the ideal source of interim labour to maintain patient care and assure the disabled dentist of income. Disability insurance will cover some of the expenses, but in most instances it is insufficient to maintain a full complement of staff. One client interviewed needed immediate surgery. The recovery period was estimated at one month. She chose to close the practice, temporarily lay off her staff, and notified the patients she would be back in a month. Her thinking was that very few, if any, patients would not be able to "wait for just one month to see me." Emergencies were referred to the local service.

She suffered a relapse and notified her staff and patients about a further delay. Sadly, her health diminished further. She had already been closed for two months! Her short-term disability insurance was about to expire. A locum was found to carry on her practice. Luckily, after this two-month closure, none of the staff had found other employment and were willing to return. Only a handful of her patients had sought another dentist and the practice was back on track within weeks. This is a fortunate situation and it was possible only due to the lack of nearby competitors. The practice was situated in a smaller community and there were limited options for the patients to seek treatment elsewhere. In a larger city, where dentists are marketing for new patients much more assertively, this practice would have suffered a substantial loss of patients in this two-month period. Too often, dentists are overly optimistic about recovery from a disability.

Those dentists born after the baby boomer era are not exempt from the locum issue. Many of this younger cohort are or have been locums or associates. Many have or will purchase their own practices and will be faced with the likelihood of needing a locum.

Dentists are advised to protect their practice and hire a locum. They can be called into service on short notice and relied upon until complete recovery occurs.

CHAPTER 7

The Preferred Model of Dental Practice: The Solo Dentist

. . . .

Why Become a Dentist?

Informal surveys and research from lectures reveal that students choose dentistry for these four reasons:

1. They want to be their own boss.
2. A family member or relative is a dentist.
3. They like to work with their hands.
4. Dentistry is a lucrative profession.

In 1916, Clapp wrote that the economic objective in practice is this:

"Men practice dentistry to earn a living and a competency. This object has been so confused with the manner of such earning that it has often been lost sight of and violent

discussions have raged about the methods employed, and left the principle untouched."

What vision do young dentists have of their practices, if the first goal is to be their own boss? ROI Corporation suggests that vision be the model of the solo practice. Experience indicates this model works best for about 75% of Canadian dentists. The rermaining 25% work within group practices, academia, public health services and professional consulting.

Why Then, Do Dentists Enter Group Practice?
Many dentists prefer to have a community of like-minded individuals who can help each other with the challenges of running the practice. They admit that they choose to be within a group for the perceived benefits of shared practice management roles. They believe that staff management, dealing with suppliers, dealing with landlords and other management issues would be best dealt with by a group.

While this has some merit, problems often arise as a result of the need for consensus within the group. Too many decision makers can be a dangerous formula.

The following scenario illustrates this fact:

"Several years ago, I helped to manage the 13-chair 8-dentist office where I practised. The financial returns were very respectable for this type of business. My accountant, however, had a different approach. He determined my net hourly income for my practice management duties.

Then he compared it to my net hourly chair-side (patient treatment) income. The two were not even close! Patient treatment was far more lucrative than the time that I spent "running the practice." This very simple demonstration changed my direction and my professional focus."

This comes from the much-noted dental expert, Dr. George Freedman.

Further study into the history of leadership reveals this:

"A multitude of rulers is not a good thing, let there be one ruler, one king."
— HOMER

Setting Up Your Practice

CHAPTER 8

Buying a Practice

• •

Who Should Set Up a New Practice?

The best candidates are those dentists without student debts, families or other financial obligations. Often they are living with parents or family and have ample free time to work evenings and weekends. Ideally, these candidates will purchase brand new equipment designed for a modern facility built to their personal specifications.

Patient flow may be scarce in the early years, and there may be long periods of downtime between patients. However, each new patient examination will be performed exactly as that dentist's unique philosophy dictates, and it is likely, with time, the practice will flourish. There will be a personal satisfaction that the practice succeeded because of the individual dentist's hard work, risk taking and decision making.

When Should a Dentist Buy a Practice?

Based on hundreds of interviews with young buyers, new graduates are likely to work in three to five different practices before reaching the stage when they are ready to buy. They may buy the practice they are working in, or another on the open market. In both cases, it will take time and patience to find the right practice. Too often, dentists buy the first practice offered to them and later admit they may have bought the wrong practice.

While young dentists must have patience in order to find their ideal practice, research suggests that dentists who purchase a practice at a younger age do financially better than those who wait.

When Is the Best Time to Buy a Dental Practice?

Buyers should be patient. Many factors come into play. A high level of clinical competency and confidence is required to start a solo practice. Secure financial backing has to be in place. Lenders will provide this only if the applying dentist is judged competent and has at least three to five years of experience.

Even if the above criteria are met, the right practice may not exist at the time. The location for a new office must be right. Competition is often fierce for an ideal office location. Landlords relate that they often have multiple bids for an office in a prime location. Successful established dental practices with a preferred office site can also have multiple bids, especially in the major cities.

Where Is the Best Place to Buy a Practice?

ROI Corporation has examined the financial statements of almost 10,000 dental practices.

In the ROI Corporation database, the top earner grossed in excess of $5.0 million and retained almost $2.0 million on an adjusted cash flow basis. This individual studied many other top performers to learn how to treat patients with the most extensive care, including implantology and various full mouth restoration techniques. Not every dentist will have the desire to be at this level, but it is achievable.

Naturally, the new patient flow and the nature of his patients contributed to his success and he could not have reached this level without possessing a certain level of charisma to gain the trust and confidence of his patients.

Some may be shocked to learn that this dentist is located in a rural town, situated several hours outside of a major Canadian city. At first glance, one may assume the patients, being rural people, could not possibly support these figures. The opposite appears to be true. These patients, having a more relaxed lifestyle, have more free time, ample ability to pay and can afford extensive treatments due to lower lifestyle costs. Some believe that big-city patients have more income, and this may be true, but with that comes increased living expenses and lifestyle habits.

Rural patients are very well informed of the need for dental care and often make ideal candidates for dentists to treat. They have a desire for increased cosmetics. Unfortunately, many of today's younger dentists fail to recognize this fact.

Data derived from ROI Corporation appraisals suggest that the incomes of the rural dentists are increasing disproportionately compared to urban-based dentists. There are several reasons for this:

- The competition in rural areas is measurably lower.
- Overhead costs are lower as rents and wages average in the lower range.
- The patients have more free time and fewer demands for other lifestyle expenditures — housing is less costly and rural families tend to purchase fewer "conspicuous" items such as luxury cars and homes.

Despite these advantages, many young dentists interviewed report that they still want to set up practices in urban areas. They want to be near cultural centres, entertainment, friends and family. Many other factors, often personal and unique to the individual dentists, prevent them from venturing out to the rural areas. This is true in all provinces and it will probably remain this way for the foreseeable future as more and more females and ethnically diverse dentists enter the profession.

It's ironic that as the need for dentists increases in rural areas, there are fewer and fewer dentists seeking to locate there. The law of supply and demand will then dictate that the rural dentists, lacking in nearby competitors, will be able to increase their fees — within reason — and can demand fees that are higher than those suggested by the dental associations. When combined with the lower overheads, this will result in even higher earnings for rural dentists. An abundance of patients will also allow them to eliminate advertising and other promotional costs, thus reducing overhead costs further.

As of 2015, it is likely that the typical rural dentist will have annual gross income exceeding one million dollars and that overheads will be no more than 50% of gross.

It would seem prudent for new dentists to closely examine the advantages inherent in a rural practice.

The Form of Ownership

The ideal structure for owning a dental practice is a professional corporation. Only recently has this practice been allowed and now most dentists in Canada form a corporation and transfer their assets to that company. There are numerous benefits, including sharing of profits with family members (usually dividends) and the ability to sell your practice with greatly reduced income tax consequences.

As of 2015, each owner of a Canadian corporation is allowed up to $813,600 in tax-free capital gains for the sale of qualified shares in a corporation. When selling, it is advisable for dentists to incorporate, if they have not already done so. When buying a practice, the same advice is true — mostly for the ongoing tax benefits of distributing dividends to family and the ability to form an independent pension plan for the dentist.

There are many other reasons and exceptional circumstances that make incorporation beneficial. An accountant should always be consulted for tax matters.

Be patient, the right opportunity will come along eventually.

CHAPTER 9

Choosing and Setting
Up a New Practice

· ·

Until the 1970s, most graduating dentists would set up
a new practice. Dentists were in short supply in many
communities and patient flow was easy to develop.
Many retired dentists relate that they simply signed a
lease, bought some equipment and before their office
door was opened they were booked for weeks. Today,
this is a rare occurrence. The success of a new graduate setting up a practice is largely determined by
office location and good fortune.

New Practices in Retail Locations

The trend towards retail dentistry began in the 1980s.
Dr. Howard Rocket, one of the co-founders of
Tridont Dental Centers, was a pioneer in bringing
traditional dentistry to the retail environment. When
asked why he did so, he responded:

"We saw potential because a great number of people were not getting dental treatments as dentists were rarely open evenings and weekends. We sought to deliver quality dentistry, at usual fees, during hours that were accessible and convenient to the public."

Locations with high visibility, signage and exposure to traffic flow became the preferred choice of many dentists, including Tridont. Dentists have located in retail plazas in the suburbs of all major cities. Once again, the demand for prime plaza locations is high, and often the best offices are gone before the plaza opens.

Choosing to situate in retail plazas has some disadvantages:

- Rents are typically 25% to 50% higher than in professional buildings.
- Retail demands evening and weekend hours, which may present a problem in the later stages of a dentist's career.
- Retail attracts good patient flow, but may also attract less reliable patients as retail tends to attract walk-ins — patients who are not always committed to optimal dental care, but only seeking immediate relief of an emergency.
- Building a practice in a retail plaza is more costly as landlords do not offer finished space and leasehold improvements will cost at least $250 per square foot.

While retail practices are common in suburban areas, many that have opened in the last five years are struggling. The existing dentists in the community are well established and while their location may be less visible than the newer retail locations, their reputation is the key reason their patients remain loyal to them.

New housing developments attract new patients, but the new homeowners already have a dentist somewhere, and the propensity for patients to remain loyal is very high in dental practice. Appraisals reveal that retail practices reach the break-even point in year two or three. How do young dentists manage to support themselves, service student debts (if applicable), pay the rent and wages, and service the bank loan required to build and equip the retail office?

The answer is likely that they fall deeper into debt while building their dream. This can be fatal to those who have not budgeted properly. (See Appendix F, Buy Versus Set-Up Comparison, for an example of an estimate of cash flow for the typical new retail practice.) It is evident that expenses exceed incomes for at least two years, on average.

Many of those who follow this path will work in other practices as an associate, waiting for their new practice to have enough patient flow. This is not recommended. Patient flow may not be adequate to keep the new dentist busy, but by being absent he/she will be unaware of the opportunities to grow his/her practice each day.

New Practices in Non-Retail Locations

Professional buildings, renovated houses and office towers are just a few alternatives to retail locations. Today's dentists often think these are old-fashioned locales and not visible enough for patients to find them. This is not always true. Surveys reveal that the large majority of patients are attracted by referral, as opposed to location, advertising or promotions.

While many dentists continue to advertise using television, park benches, billboards, radio, direct mailings and other strategies, many older dentists reveal they wasted their hard-earned dollars on advertising when forming their practices. Research revealed that in one case a new dentist spent thousands on advertising as advised by his consultant. One year later his practice had grown by 30%. When his staff surveyed the patients as to why they chose that dental practice, over 80% replied that a friend referred them. The cost of the advertising was over $25,000! The number of new patients directly attributed to this expenditure was less than 50 (a cost of about $500 dollars per patient).

Advertising certainly can be beneficial and should not be ignored. Surveys reveal that satisfied patients provide the best "advertising" because of the high referral rate they provide.

Dental practices are no exception — referral is the best method of building a practice.

How do dentists ask for a referral from an existing patient? It's simple — just ask them! Many dentists have signs in their dental reception areas stating:

"The best compliment you can pay us is the referral of a family member or friend."

This excellent idea costs less than $50 and it works. However, not enough dentists go the extra step to reinforce the sign and actually ask for referrals. Some feel it is below their professional status to ask a patient to refer a friend. Others believe it may show weakness or give the impression they are not busy. This is erroneous thinking. Many businesses ask their clients for referrals. A typical request is as follows.

"If you are satisfied with the results please tell your colleagues about me."

Many clients accept this practice and consider it good business. Advertising and promotions have their place, but in the long run, it is this word-of-mouth referral upon which dental practices are built.

Ultimately, the non-retail location may be best for those who have the confidence and the charisma to ask for referrals. Shy dentists must rely upon non-verbal methods of attracting patients. This is appropriate and encouraged for those who are somewhat introverted. Psychological studies confirm that some dentists are just that — introverted. For them, retail may be the best option.

Other Factors

Those dentists who have a unique position because of religion, culture or ethnicity in the communities they serve should consider the non-retail location. Their ability to attract patients in relation to one or more of the above factors is enhanced. While this can be a clear advantage, it can also be a disadvantage. Sometimes they lose patients because of one or more of these factors. In addition, people of similar backgrounds often ask for and expect discounts. Research indicates that this is a common phenomenon to all ethnicities and cultures and may be a limiting factor with regard to profitability. There are many patients with limited incomes and financial pressures that deserve a break and this issue requires the dentist's best judgment.

Once the process of discounting dental fees is commenced, it will become a trademark of that practice.

Patients will tell others they can get a deal with this dentist and once the word is out, the result is a low-fee practice. Then, at some point, when the dentist attempts to establish a suitable price point for the location, the patients become upset and some will leave.

CHAPTER 10

The Size and Design
of a New Dental Office

· ·

There are many common mistakes made in the design of a dental office. The first is that the dentist rented too much space. Landlords have a vested interest in renting out larger offices. Dental equipment dealers also recommend larger offices as this allows for future equipment purchases. A single dentist should be able to operate effectively in an office of 1,000 to 1,200 square feet. Prudent dentists will sign a lease that falls within this size.

There are many examples of dental practices working profitably and effectively in 1,000 square feet, with three operatories and a compact design. In fact, there are examples of two-operatory practices occupying approximately 300 square feet that are elegant, efficient and profitable.

The temptation to oversize arises from a perceived

need for privacy, staff rooms and storage, and to accommodate patient traffic flow. These are very important matters when designing the new office. The dentist's private office should be kept to a bare minimum.

> *"Dentists spend money when they're in the private office*
> *— they make money when they're in the operatory."*
> — ROY BROWN

Dr. John Wilson, who has worked as a locum dentist in dozens of dental offices, believes that most offices lack an intelligent ergonomic design. He reports that the operator's chair, the location of instrumentation and the lighting are inadequate in most operatories. In many practices he has found that the operatory countertops are cluttered with unused equipment.

According to Dr. Wilson, many dentists like to buy expensive high-tech gadgets that take up space and often do not generate additional income. Some devices may speed delivery of care, yet others only change the form of delivery. Dentists should choose their tools carefully and conservatively. Many of the new tools and technologies should only be purchased after their worth has been proven and the practice warrants their need and is able to support them.

Roy Brown's studies with Wilson Southam from The Group at Cox Company have proven invaluable in office design. They performed "time in motion" studies of dentists at work. They filmed them for several days in order to identify inefficiencies. Then, by accident, an important observation was made when the film of the dentists working was sped up. In high speed the wasted motions and hand actions of the dentists were revealed. It was discovered that much of the dentists' time was used for repetitive motions, many of which were damaging to the dentists' hands, arms, neck and back. This finding led to the four-handed revolution (dentist and assistant) in dentistry and raised a question about office size.

What's the Right-Sized Office?
In a typical solo practice the staff consists of one full-time dental assistant, a receptionist and a hygienist. In most instances, a typical office will host a maximum of three staff, along with the dentist and two or three patients. The total number of people in a solo practice, even with family members waiting and other visitors, is usually no more than eight to ten people. An industry norm for office space design and allocation of person space is 100 to 200 square feet per person.

The typical dental operatory is about 100 to 150 square feet. Therefore, for a three-operatory practice, no more than 450 square feet is required for the operating rooms.

When you consider that three people are usually in the dentist's operatory (the dentist, assistant and patient), and the hygienist and one patient are in another, you have five people in less than 300 square feet.

The balance of the person space is for the receptionist and those waiting. When asked why she had only two chairs and a small magazine rack in her waiting room of less than 100 square feet, a dentist responded:

*"Good dentists don't keep their patients waiting, so two
chairs is all I need."*

By following the above advice, the savings (due to
the decreased rent paid) would approximate $100,000
over a 25-year period.

While sterilization and storage areas are essential,
they rarely occupy someone for more than a few min-
utes at a time. Hence, these areas should be compact and
efficient. Storage is an issue for most paper-based businesses. In order to save space and rent, dentists should
regularly cull their files of inactive patients. Most offices
now use electronic files with a suitable electronic
backup to help eliminate paper record storage.

Dave Love works with Patterson Dental, the largest
distributor of dental equipment in North America,
and says this about office design:

*"The importance of proper planning and design for a
dental office, especially within the confines of an operatory
cannot be overstated. Functionality, and economy of
motion are very important, thus eliminating time wasting
movements, and preventing injury or possible disability.
Your full-service dental dealer should be one of the first
parties you speak with when planning the build or
renovation of your dental office."*

The modern business office must accommodate
an electronic workstation. Older office designs did
not foresee the need for computers, monitors, printers
and the like, as well as the cabling required. Modern

computer furniture is ergonomically designed and hides most of the unsightly cabling. The new office must take advantage and be aware of the cutting edge furniture available.

Record Storage

The trend towards electronic records will continue to be the norm. Traditional paper files holding panoramic x-rays and the other documents employed in the past are no longer relevant. The typical office design should allow the team easy access to the digital records with no visible paper files.

As the traditional practice grew, files accumulated and became worn. With the modern computer software available, storage problems have been eliminated. However, due to the paper-based training methods of many dentists, it is likely that paper records will continue for at least another few years. However a new dental office design may contain a small, concealed and private chart and records room.

The Private Office and Staff Room

Dental office staff will need a private space to retire to for lunch and breaks. This room is often neglected in office design. It should be compact, yet comfortable and easy to keep clean and tidy. It should contain a sink, a fridge, a microwave and provisions for making tea and coffee, along with a place to sit. Providing these basics indicates the dentist's concern for the needs of his/her staff and respects their need for a private space and private time.

The dentist's own private office should be small and compact in order to keep within the overall 1,000 to 1,200 square foot office design. Time must be spent to keep this office organized and tidy. Any financial, personal or confidential papers should be under lock and key. These should be eventually removed and stored in a more secure location.

Patient interviews reveal that many patients' opinions of the dentist are based on the overall appearance and cleanliness of all aspects of the practice. They are often unaware of the strict sterilization protocols, but remember the clutter in the waiting room. They appreciate that the dentist's and the staff's credentials, educational degrees and achievements are displayed in easy view but not to excess. They can often recall any artwork that was on display.

The Waiting Room

The waiting room should have a comfortable place to wait that does not allow the patient to overhear phone conversations or the receptionist's discussions with other patients. Some current magazines and a small area with books and toys that would interest children are a nice touch. In the unlikely event that the dentist is running late, a clock should not be visible in the waiting room to avoid staff or patient stress.

The Treatment Planning Room

This room is solely for discussing complex cases and financial matters. It is essential, but again, should only be large enough to accommodate three people at a time. This allows for the person giving the treatment (not always the dentist), the patient and one family member to go over all aspects of the treatment.

Specialists, such as orthodontists, typically require larger rooms for presenting treatments. This room should be free of all clinical materials and be non-threatening in all regards. Ideally, the room should be elegant in its simplicity. Some dentists prefer to post their degrees here in order to ensure their patients know they are qualified.

Washrooms

Ideally, two bathrooms within your dental suite are best, one for patients and one for staff. Many landlords of older, existing buildings are not able to provide two bathrooms within a suite. If you are fortunate enough to secure a lease prior to final construction, then plan to install two bathrooms. Toothbrushes, mouthwash and cups are a welcome addition for patient use before treatment.

With many of the above considerations in mind, a dentist should be able to design an office that meets the criteria and remains within the 1,000 to 1,200 square foot limitation. In doing so, he or she will maximize profitability while providing for the comfort and needs of patients and staff.

Maintaining Your Dental Office

Dentists are well trained to maintain a sterile clinical space but often their front office does not project the image of cleanliness. The front of a dental practice is like a show room. It must always be clean, uncluttered and welcoming to patients. This is an opportunity to impress them. Many patients own their own businesses and may judge your clinical skills according to your office cleanliness and organization.

Once in the clinical areas, patients will notice any faults or eyesores — even in the ceiling! Dentists should sit in their patient chairs and observe what their patients are seeing. Often the ventilation ducts are dirty and ceiling tiles have unsightly water stains from condensation from the overhead pipes.

Most office cleaners are not given enough time to adequately clean an office. The typical dentist will hire a firm to clean once a week. In doing so, the cleaners are given three or four hours to perform a series of routine tasks — the floors, bathrooms and counter tops — basically they look down while they clean. Rarely do they look up or think to dust where patients look. Set out a specific, alternating cleaning schedule of specific areas for them. This may increase your weekly fees, but it is worth it.

CHAPTER 11

Financing a New or Established Practice

● ●

All of the Canadian chartered banks are interested in financing dentists. They know that a dental practice is a wise investment and regularly provide term loans and lines of credit to get them started. In some instances, they will consolidate student loans into the total loan amount to allow for efficient cash flow management. When starting up a new practice they sometimes ask for additional security, over and above the equipment and leaseholds, to secure their loan.

Leasing companies also provide financing for start-up, typically at slightly higher interest rates, although they usually do not ask for additional security. Most leasing companies do not offer lines of credit for initial operating costs, thus new dentists often seek a line of credit from a bank or trust company.

Leasing allows for accelerated tax deductions,

versus the traditional method of depreciating equipment over longer periods of time.

Lease Versus Loan — Which Should You Choose?

Most accountants suggest that the choice between a lease and a loan is dependent upon your individual circumstances. Loan payments, while usually based on a lower interest rate, typically require higher monthly payments, as they do not provide for a buyout at the end of the term. Leases usually offer lower monthly payments, with a lump sum (usually 10% of the original cost) payable at the end of the lease, when you have completed the payment schedule.

Go to www.ethiclease.com and use the lease calculator to determine the exact payment schedule. In order to calculate the actual monthly costs, new dentists will require the following information:

1. The amount they intend to borrow
2. The interest rate demanded by the leasing company (most will provide this rate, although some rely upon a "rate factor" which is not an interest rate — it is only a convenient multiplier)
3. The length of the lease (typically 60 or 84 months)
4. The buyout at the end of the lease (usually 10% of the original amount borrowed)

Once these figures are input, the calculator will prepare an amortization schedule showing the precise monthly payment, the principal and the interest cost each month, and the total amount to be paid, including interest.

It's important to know that leasing companies charge sales taxes (PST, GST or HST) on each payment, while bank loans require payment of the sales taxes up front. This usually requires immediate use of part of the line of credit — something some accountants advise against.

Other sources for comparing lease versus loan are:

- www ethiclease.com
- www.sinclairdental.com (click on the financial services icon)
- All Canadian chartered banks have lease versus loan calculators on their websites

Before choosing which is the best financing option, new dentists should consult their accountant.

Buying an Established Practice

The chartered banks are the best choice for the purchase of a practice with existing cash flow. They usually offer term loans at the prevailing prime rate of interest, plus 0.5% to 1%. A sample loan proposal can be obtained from almost any bank. Since an established practice has a proven track record, you can usually negotiate more favourable terms with the banks as compared to financing a new start-up.

While very few dentists actually declare bankruptcy in Canada each year (the rate of bankruptcy for dentists is well below the norm for other businesses), banks are conservative by nature and often request a complete business plan for the new start-up loan application. This plan takes considerable work, as it must be well documented and supported by competition overviews and a demographic analysis of the planned location.

A young dentist, interviewed a few years ago, prepared an elaborate business plan based on extensive research, and successfully obtained a bank loan to set up a brand new retail dental office. He opened up a beautiful new office within nine months, proudly inviting many guests to the opening ceremony. The office was modern, well designed and situated in a high-growth area.

The office had room for five operatories that he chose to fully equip from the beginning. Although he knew that he did not have enough patients to justify equipping five operatories, the price was favourable because he was buying in quantity. Unfortunately, his growth was a little slower than budgeted, and the loan payments, when combined with high rent (due to the high-profile retail location he selected) and staff wages, exceeded the monthly cash flow for the first few years.

Fortunately, he did not have large personal debts, as he was single and living at home with parents. To make ends meet he began working as an associate in another office. His absence from his own practice at this crucial time of development further aggravated his problems.

The lesson here is obvious — do not borrow too much too soon. New practices require constant attention and full-time attendance. A new practice should start with one or two fully equipped operatories. As the practice grows and cash flow increases, new operatories can be added. New dentists should resist the temptation to secure discounts for bulk purchases.

CHAPTER 12

Buying an Established Practice, and Clinical Compatibility

• •

Who Should Buy a Practice?

The ability to secure a list of patients is the primary reason to buy a practice. Dentists with large student loans, families, mortgages and other debts should seriously consider associating for a longer period, or they should investigate the purchase of an established practice with existing cash flow. Some argue that delaying ownership conflicts with their desire to be their own boss. The delay is unavoidable for some, often for financial reasons. Others feel that if they buy a practice they will not have the new equipment and décor they desire. The cosmetic elements of a practice are easily modified over time.

One compromise is that the philosophy of the previous owner is well entrenched in the minds of the staff and patients, and a sudden change can be upsetting. When buying a patient list, dentists should consider the following:

Make as few major changes as possible for the first year.

Once the dentist has introduced him/herself to the patients and met with them at least twice, they will be relatively comfortable with the dentist. This usually takes about two recall appointments, or about one year. At this point, the cash flow will be consistent, and any modifications the dentist wishes to implement will be more easily accepted and should be more affordable.

For dentists purchasing an established practice, the most important consideration is to find an office where the clinical philosophy is similar to their own. Two like-minded dentists will easily transition a practice from one to the other.

How Do You Determine Clinical Compatibility?

Most dental practices for sale do not allow the prospective buyers to work in the office prior to an offer having been made. Owners want to keep the sale of their practice confidential. If more than one prospective buyer is allowed to "test drive" the practice, confusion for both patients and staff results, and invariably production drops.

Owners are certainly not interested in losing income as the prospective buyer makes up his/her mind. There are consultants who promote the "hire your buyer" theory, which means that the most serious candidate is allowed to work in the practice prior to making their offer. This has merit, but mostly benefits the buyer. The owner is kept in a state of anxiety while the young, less-experienced dentist examines every aspect of the practice. Often, this can generate negative side effects that can damage the goodwill value of a practice. In the end, it is best to avoid hiring the prospective buyer.

How Do You Determine Whether a Practice Matches Your Clinical Philosophy if You Cannot See Patients and Work with the Staff?
This can be ascertained by examining the following:

- *The method of scheduling* — How much time is being allotted for various procedures reveals the style and skills of the dentist and the practice's main sources of income.
- *The equipment, supplies and materials used* — The technique of one dentist is easily determined when another examines their instruments, materials and operatory set up.
- *The overall décor and layout of the office* — A thorough inspection of all the facilities often reveals much about the personality of the selling dentist and the overall makeup of the practice.

While the above considerations may seem obtuse, it is important to remember that in the past dentists often never met until an offer was agreed upon. Today, most qualified buyers are permitted the opportunity to meet the owner and make an initial examination of the premises before making an offer.

The practice of keeping the buyer uninformed about the staff and patients is in place for a reason — you are buying a business, not people. Although the list is the business asset that is being sold, meeting the patients does not alter the view of most buyers, as they admit that they simply want a list of patients to treat.

Other characteristics of the patients are easily determined with the aid of modern computers. The ethnicity is easily found by examining charts that contain last names. Most computer systems can also generate geographic profiles: for example, where the patients come from. Some can even prepare insured-versus-uninsured patient reports.

It is much easier today for an owner to educate a buyer about his/her practice. Buyers can be confident that they will be able to determine the style and modalities of practice, and, most importantly, the clinical philosophy of the owner without the need to meet the owner or to work in the practice.

STRATEGIES FOR MANAGING STAFF

CHAPTER 13

Running a
Dental Practice

• •

The greatest management challenge dentists face is managing people. Staff, patients, suppliers and lab technicians can be the most demanding and unpredictable part of a day, yet they are the most critical element of the business. Dentists relate that they are well trained to provide dental care but often struggle with their people skills.

How Can Dentists Develop Their People Skills?
Older dentists relate that these skills are developed with time, trial and error. Once in practice, they were faced with handling numerous daily tasks influenced by people's fears, objections, emotions and perceived needs. Many dentists relate that dealing with their staff is even more difficult than handling their patients. There are individual differences in the staff-dentist

relationships, as well as in inter-staff relationships. Both have to be overseen by the dentist.

Interviews reveal that most dentists have not written or purchased an office policy manual. They admit that they rely on advice gathered informally from their colleagues and third-party advisors. There are many well-conceived office manuals available, yet few dentists believe these standard references are appropriate for their unique style of management.

Dentists who do not have an office manual, whether purchased or self-written, do so at their own peril. The manual provides a starting point for both the dentist and his/her staff. It can avoid many potential problems and expedite many that arise.

The manual should be an ever-changing document that is modified as time goes by and good business practices change. Staff should be reminded regularly of office policies and updated on all changes made.

Associates should learn from their principal's successes or failures, and develop their own unique model. Once in ownership, new ideas can be tried and their outcomes analyzed in order to build a manual that works. Templates for dental practice manuals are available and many courses are offered that provide guidelines. Over time, an office manual will become an integral part of the dentist's practice and reflect the needs of the dentist, staff and patients.

More on Staff Relations

Dentist interviews reveal this common query:

"What if they don't like me?"

While being liked by staff is important, it should not be an obsession, and many dentists miscalculate what their relationship with their staff should be. The staff's first priority is to be employed in a job for which they are trained and suitably qualified. Secondly, and not to be underestimated, is that all employees want to work in an environment where they feel needed and are respected by all other people in the workplace.

In many cases the staff are somewhat indifferent to the owner, as long as they have learned to get along with him/her. It is often the other staff that cause the unsettling moments of tension within the office.

Assembling a team of like-minded individuals who trust and respect each other is of greater importance than hiring staff that like the dentist.

Many speakers on staff relations talk and write about people working in harmony toward a higher and often lofty goal. This is an excellent concept and one that people should strive for. The reality is that staff are more often there for income and security reasons, rather than the contrived ideals of management experts.

Dentists should respect and reward their staff for their work performance. They should be kind and thoughtful employers, but they should not attempt to be their employees' best friend.

In 1916, Clapp wrote:

"A most disagreeable feature of young lady assistants is that many of them regard 'the job' as merely a stepping stone from school to the altar."

Of course, the quote is dated and patriarchal; but, for many working in a dental office is temporary and not a long-term career choice. Many of today's assistants aspire to be a dental hygienist or to move on to other pursuits. Dentists would be wise to understand this.

CHAPTER 14

Selecting a
Business System

● ●

How do you run a dental practice? Business systems are the tools of managing the flow of information. Today, computers perform most of the functions, yet people are the ones who enter and manage the data.

Modern software has an incredible capability to deliver crucial data. One mistake made by many dentists is that they do not understand their software and leave this task to their staff. In doing so dentists are in danger of losing control that may lead to employee misappropriation of money. Fraud is evident in all businesses, and dentistry is no exception. There are courses that can be taken to help identify and prevent fraud, but the central problem is that the dentist does not understand the software system or how to control cash flow. It is very easy to alter entries and delete charges once a patient has paid.

A recent case involved a dentist who was the victim of theft exceeding $200,000. He had a very loyal receptionist who always looked after all his finances — both business and personal. She had systematically stolen small amounts daily for over 15 years.

She was able to pull this off for years until a new banker at his branch performed a random review of several clients' depositing practices. In an attempt to reduce the dentist's monthly bank fees, his banker noticed dual accounts — one for the dentist, one for her. At first he was furious, then he felt humiliated and sank into a mild depression. How could she do that to him after all those years? She was relieved of her position and he had no choice but to sue. A small amount was recovered and he is still in practice, but he claims he still feels demoralized.

The lesson to be learned for dentists is not to be overly trusting. One person should never be allowed to control business and personal finances and to perform all the tasks of billing, collecting, depositing and managing the practice's funds.

Many dentists employ a spouse or family member to supervise this essential aspect of business ownership. Others use a third party, a bookkeeper who is only involved in preparing payables and financial reports.

One key indicator that staff members may be committing fraud is that they refuse to take holidays. They must remain on the job constantly to keep their system of fraud concealed. If you have a staff member, who handles billing or collections and he/she never takes a holiday, be warned.

CHAPTER 15

Staff Wages and Bonus Systems

• •

Dentists have employed many types of bonus systems as incentives for staff to reach higher levels of performance. A bonus system is a great idea and experience suggests the following:

- Bonuses should be not be allocated at pre-set times.
- Bonuses should be immeasurable by staff.

They should never be tied to specific dates, events, anniversaries or factors that lead a staff member to conclude that they are more or less automatic.

One exception that seems to prevail for many is a bonus at Eid, Hanukkah, or Christmas time. Another exception to the rule occurs when a long-standing tradition has been established in the practice that would be both difficult and unwise to eliminate.

Staff should be apprised when business is good but not be made aware of all financial statements. Performance bonuses should be paid on a random, ever-changing timetable. When bonuses are distributed, all that needs to be said is as follows:

"Lately we have done well, thank you for a job well done!"

In this way, the dentist remains in control of the bonus system. The bonus amount can and probably should vary from employee to employee. Staff members are unique and so are their levels of effectiveness, contribution and seniority. As much as possible, each bonus should be kept confidential to avoid staff jealousy and unnecessary questioning about the rationale for bonus amounts.

Initially, there is little that can be done if staff members choose to reveal their earnings and/or the amount of their bonuses. If this becomes problematic, then staff should be confronted individually and made aware of office policies that discourage sharing such information. If need be, justification for such policies should be made on the basis that only the dentist has all the facts necessary to make determinations on wages and bonuses.

Many experts and dentists argue for a system that is more transparent. Some offices actually post daily, weekly and monthly income information in a staff room. Staff become aware of income statements, wages paid and bonuses given. The belief is that by having all information available to everyone, productivity will increase.

Experience has shown that the transparent model is more likely to lead to unnecessary and counterproductive questioning of the dentist's rationale and decision-making skills. In addition, greed, jealousy and resentment are often by-products.

Dentists are advised to keep their financial statements private for the most part. Some statistics should be shared with staff, such as total patients seen in a day, or the occasional monthly objective, such as keeping collections to a certain level of production. This is a good business practice because it is inclusive just as it is necessary to inform staff when things are not up to the dentist's standards.

Some Pitfalls to Avoid

One dentist interviewed revealed that his staff knew everything because of the records on the office computer. He was asked the following:

"Do your staff know all of the expenses of your practice?"

He readily admitted that they did not, and he also went on to say that he was earning much less than his staff thought. He was embarrassed to tell his staff how high the overhead was, and he wanted to maintain the image of a successful dentist. This position, while honourable, left him to pay higher wages than the industry norm.

He was advised by a consultant that staff should cost

between 28% and 32% of total billings — so he always paid wages and bonuses that equalled that amount by the end of the year. Staff cost analysis revealed he was paying substantially higher wages.

The lesson here is that guidelines and consultant advice can be misleading. Dentists should pay what is fair for their area and their marketplace.

One dentist made a habit of hiring young, inexperienced people for low wages. He took great time to train them and to teach them his methods of running a dental practice. His total wages, when divided into his gross income, were 11%. If he had used the guideline of the consultants, he would have paid out another 20% of his gross income just to be in line with industry averages. The competency of such workers was not a question as they were well trained. They were respected, tutored in dental work, and adequately compensated. They enjoyed their position in the practice.

The highest wages, as a percentage of gross, are usually found in the newer practices, and most often in the new start-up practice. When gross is small due to limited patient flow, wages can be as much as 50% of billings. When all remaining expenses are paid, the owners discover they have subsidized the practice for one or two years. Once a practice has surpassed the break-even point, wages should fall in line with the Canadian industry norm of 28% to 32% of gross. (See Appendix F, Buy Versus Set-Up Comparison.) There will always be exceptions, and one or two percentage points should not measure success. The key to remember is that practices can be run on low wages as long as staff are well trained and those wages are viable in the marketplace in which the practice is run. Dental associations, dental study clubs, appraisers and consultants often make this information available for a fee.

One client indicated that his bonus system was based on the number of new patient exams performed each month. He set a base number of 25 new exams per month; each one thereafter earned a specified amount that was pooled and distributed to staff at the end of the month, based on seniority. This sounds simple enough. However, he was distraught to learn that for many years several of the staff had been booking phantom patients into the system to increase the numbers. The dentist was a kind, trusting man, and given his busy schedule and personal obligations, he never went back each month to verify that the new patient exams were actually performed. He trusted the computer reports and his staff. He had paid out bonuses (most of which were legitimately payable to the staff) in excess of $25,000. In particular, he noticed that the receptionist had entered many false names to increase her bonus by $100 per month. Had he made a bonus system that was not pre-set in times given and immeasurable, this would not have occurred.

CHAPTER 16

Benefits and Performance Reviews

• •

Other than the mandatory payment of CPP, EI, and vacation pay of 4%, many dentists do not offer benefits. Dentists typically offer free dental care to staff and their families, paid professional development courses, and other "perks." Traditionally, a benefits package was not offered because the plans were too expensive, with steep premiums to businesses with fewer than 25 employees. Some dentists felt that they wanted to keep their business plan simple, cost efficient and that staff turnover negated the need for a benefits package. Today, many insurance companies offer small business benefits plans (from 3 to 50 employees) that are more affordable.

It is the individual dentist's choice to offer benefits. Some dentists believe that the best benefit you can offer staff is a higher wage for a job well done, however many surveys show that benfits, recognition and team spirit is important to employees.

Performance Reviews
"An order that can be misunderstood will be misunderstood."
— Napoleon Bonaparte

When assessing performance, dentists are reminded that they are responsible for the direction given to staff. Staff can only perform as instructed or as requested, and rarely will they exceed expectations — it's the nature of the employee mentality.

Most business owners dread the annual review process. It is an old custom that has merit, but it causes the staff and the owner anxiety. Research suggests the best way to review the performance of a staff member is the continuous method. When someone performs well, let them know — recognition is one of the top three reasons people enjoy their jobs.

When employees perform poorly, inform them immediately. There is no advantage in waiting. A clear, gentle suggestion as to expectations is required; then move on. When employment anniversaries arrive, you can offer staff an increase in wage without the stressful review of the past mistakes. Successful dentists rarely hold a meeting with a staff member on his/her anniversary to review shortcomings; they mostly want to reward staff for another year of loyalty and to offer them an increase in wage.

How Much Should You Increase Wages?

Wages are an important measurement of an individual's "worth" in the market. Once a starting wage is established most employees will expect an increase each year. Most dentists will follow the cost of living index as published by the Government of Canada (www. statcan.gc.ca). There are ample references to cost of living indexes on the Internet. They measure the effective increase in the costs of running a household for the average Canadian. Unfortunately, if this is the only increase given, it does not reward for increased performance or seniority. This only allows an increase for the Cost of Living Allowance (COLA). Our research suggests adding 1% or 2% to the COLA is fair.

Wages should increase by no more than 5% in a stable economy, and perhaps marginally lower in times of low inflation. After 5, 10, or 15 years, many dentists offer additional bonuses for seniority such as additional vacation pay above and beyond the mandatory 4%.

One client, a generous man, offers 6% vacation pay after five years and 8% after ten years. Each 2% increase in vacation pay is equal to one week's paid vacation. Therefore, 4% equals two weeks, 6% equals three weeks and 8% equals four weeks. Most employers do not exceed 8% as it is impractical to allow the employee more than one month off — it is too disruptive to workflow and the practice becomes far too reliant upon temporary staff.

CHAPTER 17

Employment Contracts and Staff Dismissal

· ·

Should you put staff on written contracts? Historically, it wasn't necessary. Today, this is why it's absolutely essential: laws that are increasingly pro-employee; employees who have been made rights-savvy through the Internet; increased litigiousness from contingency fees; and the increased wealth of dentists, which makes them targets. Today, practising without written contracts would be as foolhardy as practising without malpractice insurance. Consider two key factors when hiring an expert on employment law: (1) they should be very familiar with dental practice purchase and sale agreements and not have any conflict of interest in providing both legal advice and brokerage advice, and (2) they should have empirical knowledge of employment law and how these two aspects of a practice sale are managed by the broker. The expectations of all the parties to the sale often differ as to how each process will be managed with respect to timing and notifications to staff. If you take just one thing away from this book, please talk to a broker as to how this is handled.

The most contentious issue arising in the modern dental practice is the non-solicitation clause. Essentially, this clause restricts an employee from contacting patients in the event he/she quits or is dismissed from a practice. Hygienists have the greatest influence in this regard and many dentists are concerned that they may attract patients to a nearby competitor. The hygienist has more contact with patients than the dentist in many instances and often develops a stronger relationship with the patients.

When hiring a new hygienist, it is not unreasonable to ask her/him to sign a contract. For existing hygienists in the practice, asking them to sign a contract with a non-solicitation clause will cause them to fear for the security of their position — they will assume that dismissal is pending. While this may not be the dentist's intention, it will likely be the perception of a long-standing staff member. One client attended a Friday morning seminar about employment issues and was supplied with a sample employment contract. He returned to his practice on Monday morning and delivered a copy to each staff member suggesting this was now the industry norm for dental offices. He was confident they would comply, since they had worked well together for years. He thought little of the matter until later that week when the staff approached him as a group. They promptly announced they would not sign the contract and that another dentist in the area had offered to hire each of them — without the need to sign any contracts! He was shocked that his staff of many years would threaten such actions, and quickly agreed to drop the whole idea. Then conditions got worse. The staff demanded increases in their wages, to match what the other dentist had offered, or they would all quit! Once again, he was shocked, and fearful for the continuity of his practice.

What was the end result? He gave them all raises, never obtained one signature, and his staff remained demoralized. Then he began running classified ads for new staff and as the resumés started coming in, the staff assumed they were all being replaced. Two of them quit within weeks, and he fired two others within a few months. His gross income dropped substantially and patients began to question his ability to run a business when he had such a high staff turnover. One of the hygienists eventually found a position with a nearby competitor, and because of her distaste for the former dentist, she made every effort to contact as many patients as she could find. In fact, it was rumoured that she had retained her day sheets for several months before leaving, and they contained not only names, but also phone numbers! While this was never proven, one can imagine the damage done to a practice if hundreds of patients begin to seek treatment elsewhere.

All this was a result of an "expert" at the Friday morning seminar suggesting these contracts were necessary to protect this dentist's business!

In summary, dentists should be very careful when addressing this topic, especially with existing staff members.

Dismissing a Staff Member

Many dentists and business owners tell of the trauma they experienced when letting staff go. This is probably one of the most difficult tasks dentists have to do.

Some words of advice:

- Obtain proper advice from an employment specialist — usually a lawyer.
- Document everything!
- Do it sooner rather than later!

Rarely does a bad employment situation get better. Many business owners feel obligated toward their employees. They often feel guilty. Dentists must remember that they have obligations to their own practice, their staff, their family and the industry as a whole. In these matters it is essential to act with decency and to be gentle but firm.

Dentists should record every event that has transpired. This gives them the rationale for dismissing a staff member. These records should document the employee's incompetence or the actions contrary to office policies and job descriptions.

One dentist related that he was unaware of the actions a staff member was taking because he did not work directly with her. She had been openly criticizing other staff in the presence of the patients. It was discovered when a close friend who was also a patient finally told the dentist that his long-term staff member was making derogatory racial remarks about another staff member. This was unacceptable, and he was forced to dismiss her. Unfortunately, he had no proof, as the other staff members would not admit to or verify the racial slurs — likely for fear of the repercussions. He chose not to mention the racial issue when dismissing her, using the poorly disguised excuse that she was not performing her tasks adequately. The problem was that she was actually very good at her job. After being released, she sought the advice of a labour law specialist who informed her that she had been wrongfully dismissed, whereby she sued the dentist. He never gave any evidence about the true reason she was dismissed, and he lost the case, resulting in a payment to her of almost one year's wages. The message here is to document everything, record the facts, obtain staff testimonials (where possible) and act decisively.

CHAPTER 18

Workplace Harassment and Staff Training

• •

Unfortunately, there are instances where the dentist may be responsible for some form of harassment of the staff. Dentistry can be stressful, and on occasion dentists vent their frustrations on the staff. This can be prevented by recognizing that staff are one of the greatest influences on the overall business performance. In many instances, harassment issues can be avoided by stepping back and taking a long, sober pause. Things often look different after a good night's sleep.

Today, workplace harassment laws are clearer in definition and are intended to provide protection for both employees and employers. In many cases they have altered the workplace environment and dynamics. Dentists should be aware of these laws, which are periodically updated. In Ontario and many other provinces, all employers must have a workplace harassment policy regardless of the size of the work-place and the number of employees.

From the early 1900s to the 1960s, most dentists were male and their staff were, and still are, female. Given the close proximity in which dentists and their staff work, it is understandable that "accidental intimacies" (a ROI corporation term) resulted.

> *The most costly business decision you will ever make is to have an office affair — especially if you're married!*

ROI Corporation has been retained to perform hundreds of appraisals as a result of matrimonial break-down. In some instances, the office romance was the reason for the divorce. The effects on the business are often disastrous. Office tensions soar as a result of the changed dynamics, and business invariably suffers, at least for a time. While many of these "accidental intimacies" lead to long-term successful relationships, it is strongly recommended that dentists avoid them.

Staff Training

Most dentists pay for staff to attend industry conventions and seminars. Their wages are paid for the time spent, and course fees are usually paid as well. Others pay only the wage, and ask the staff to pay for the continuing education — a practice that is unfair and leads to resentment. If staff are sent to a course or convention, even if it's deemed to be "fun," they should be paid both their wages and all other related costs, with the exception of meals.

There are many courses offered by a wide variety of experts on staff morale, office functionality, increasing performance and other important topics. Both dentists and staff should attend these regularly. One client sent his entire team to a highly respected program promising to increase income and profitability of the practice. He did not attend. When the staff returned, they were full of new ideas and concepts that they wanted to implement. He allowed them to proceed, only to discover that the tactics were not in keeping with his philosophy. Yes, the methods employed were being used in other dental offices, and they did indeed increase production — but at what cost?

The assertive tactics of the staff offended some long-standing patients, as they suggested that more dentistry was needed than the dentist had recommended. The experts had told the staff about a treatment planning method that would persuade patients to accept more treatments. Staff want to be on a winning team, one that succeeds and that will eventually be able to afford to pay higher wages. However, dentists should be very careful about the courses they send staff to, and should attend with them to be sure what they are learning is consistent with the dentist's overall philosophy.

OPTIMIZING SUCCESS

CHAPTER 19

Secrets of a Successful Practice

The top three secrets to success in dental practice are:

1. Be patient focused first and foremost.
2. Respect and recognize your staff.
3. Do not be afraid to say "no thank you" to sales people if you are not clear about the benefits of their products.

Patients are the only source of income for the practice. They should be cared for in a fashion that reflects appreciation of their trust and confidence. As previously discussed, many dentists have difficulty relating to and conversing with their patients. Dentists must make every effort to develop people and conversational skills in order to have a genuine relationship with patients. This may require attendance at seminars designed for this purpose and a constant awareness of this personal need.

Why Do Patients Remain Loyal to Their Dental Office?
There are five key reasons patients return to your practice (in order of importance):

1. *Location* — proximity to work or home
2. *Staff* — familiar and friendly people
3. *Policies* — patients know what to expect
4. *The Dentist* — a trusted source of care
5. *Habit* — people do not like change, particularly with health care providers

While many argue that patients return primarily for the dentist, research suggests that this is the fourth most important reason. There are thousands of cases on record where dentists have been successfully replaced by new, and often younger, dentists.

What Happens When There Is a Change in Dentist?
ROI Corporation surveys indicate the two key statistics that prevail every time a dental practice is sold:

1. 85% to 95% of the patients return within a year, even when their dentist of many years retires.
2. Revenues increase 5% to 15% within one year.

This would suggest that while there are many loyalties to a dental practice, these are not necessarily attributed to the dentist.

Why Does the Income Go Up Within the First Year?

Young dentists are determined to repay student or bank loans. They also bring new ideas, energy and drive to the practice. They are highly motivated and will almost always outperform the previous dentist. The new dynamic and the energy flow created are reflected in staff revitalization and patient curiosity to meet the new dentist. There is a new buzz in the practice, and increased production is often the result.

The new dentist is often trained in procedures that were previously referred out. Many of today's young buyers with three to five years of experience have taken courses in endodontics, orthodontics and implant surgery. While they are still relatively new to the profession, many are more than capable, and with the aid of modern tools and techniques, they are performing a wider array of treatments compared to the last generation of general dentists. This increases production substantially in some instances.

One practice examined was performing only the regular recall appointments and simple restorative work. The dentist was capable; he just did not like the long appointments and the stress of surgery or complicated dentistry. He was referring out all his endodontics, surgery, orthodontics and even some crown and bridge work — the favourite of most dentists. He admitted that he was very conservative and many of his patients were in need of extensive treatments. Within one year of a new dentist taking over, revenues almost doubled from $600,000 to well over $1,000,000!

The new owner related that she found the transition

very easy since patients actually wanted more extensive treatments, but mentioned that they did not want to question the judgment of or to insult their former dentist by suggesting he was not meeting their needs. Most patients are very understanding and trust their dentist. In today's society, patients are demanding a wider scope of options from their dentist.

The proliferation of cosmetics, mostly for baby boomers, is a dentist's dream come true. Witness the TV shows that promote complete makeovers and you will see that cosmetic dental enhancement is almost always part of the process. This trend, while appearing to be superficial or temporary, is likely to last for at least another 20 years while the boomer generation continues to improve their physical appearance.

Managing your Overhead

The top four expenses in every dental practice are:

1. Wages
2. Supplies
3. Laboratory
4. Rent

For solo dental practices, the average portion of total revenue spent is:

1. Wages — 28% to 32%
2. Supplies — 5% to 8%
3. Lab — 4% to 7%
4. Rent — 3% to 6%

Much has been said about keeping costs in check, and the best-run practices track their monthly and annual expenses with ease. Cash flow analysis and control is not as difficult as some believe; it's simply the art of recording the expenses, tracking them over specified time periods and measuring the results against the trend in total income.

There are many systems for charting your individual expenses, usually with the aid of a spreadsheet program such as Microsoft Excel, and with regular input, the top four expenses can be monitored.

Dentists often turn to third parties for help with the task of understanding their overhead (more often than is necessary at times). Experts who analyze financial statements are readily available, but many dentists perform their own analysis and believe it allows them better control of their finances.

CHAPTER 20

Advertising and Income Hours in the Dental Practice

. . . .

In the early 1980s, a challenge was made to the rules governing dental professionals' advertising tactics. Until then, most regulatory bodies permitted a dentist to post signs of no more than four inches in height, and the practice of advertising was strictly controlled and even classified as "professional misconduct" by some. After a lengthy battle, the courts ruled that dentists should be allowed to advertise much like traditional business owners. The gates had been opened, and all forms of advertising and promotion ensued.

A glance at today's telephone directories anywhere in Canada reveals a major trend toward aggressive marketing. Dentists are using sophisticated and effective colour ads to promote their practices.

As well, in every major city, dentists can be seen advertising on roadside billboards, park benches, neon signs, radio, TV and other media. Dentists have been forced to be more creative and have used a variety of promotions to set themselves apart from the rest of the competition.

One client related that he spends over $20,000 per month on various forms of advertising, resulting in a higher than average new patient flow. He went on to suggest that many of those he attracts from his sophisticated marketing are not the ideal patients for his philosophy, but he believes that if only 10% of those who inquire are accepting of his comprehensive treatment planning, it's money well spent.

Extensive advertising and promotion is necessary only for some dentists, namely those in the early stages of practice. As the patient base grows, dependence on marketing tactics should decrease. For the new practice owner, a budget of 2% to 5% of income is sufficient for ads and promotions. As the practice flourishes, this budget can be reduced to 1% to 3%. Once dentists have reached the point where they are fully booked for two to four weeks in advance, there is a temptation to reduce or eliminate ads and promotions. In fact, many dentists who completely eliminate their marketing budgets report little negative effect on their practices.

The established dentist, with 1,000 patients or more, needs little help to attract new patients. Referral will generate new patient flow of about 10 to 20 patients a month in most practices. Even after factoring in a patient attrition rate of 1% to 2% a year, a dentist's referral network will almost certainly result in an adequate patient base.

ROI Corporation databases indicate some interesting figures about patient count and average income per patient per year. For example, many dentists are now generating over $1,000 per year per "active" patient. In Canada, the typical active patient is now spending about $600–$700 per year on dental care. Therefore, the average Canadian dentist needs only 700–800 patients to earn about $500,000 per year in fees. There are many exceptions, such as young children, who have less need. Those dentists situated in low-income neighbourhoods, may require up to 1,500 active patients to earn a similar income, and dentists in high-income areas may be satisfied with as few as 500.

Income Hours

It is essential that dentists track their actual income hours and the resulting fees generated. Income hours refer to the hours spent at chair-side treating patients. Hours spent performing management duties are not included. The young dentist will work 1,500 to 2,000 chair-side hours, and should generate about $350 per hour, given today's fee guides. This will result in dental fees of $400,000–$600,000 per year. As dentists become more experienced and their skills and efficiency improve, it's not uncommon to reach hourly production figures of $500–$700 per hour, depending on the type of treatments performed. Some dentists, who have taken extensive clinical and continuing education courses, generate in excess of $1,000 per hour.

However, due to the long appointments required

to generate higher hourly fees, they typically see fewer patients per day, thus allowing them to rely upon a lower active base. One of the drawbacks of their increasing hourly production is the propensity to reduce the ongoing needs of those patients. As the treatment plan reaches completion, patients' average annual spending will decrease as they enter the maintenance phase of their care. Dentists then become reliant upon their referral network. They may even resort to advertising and promotions once again, to renew adequate new patient flow and sustain their income expectation.

This process can become cyclical. Income increases, patient flow decreases; income declines and dentists seek to increase flow again. Many dentists suffer from this phenomenon, and it is a natural evolution through the mid-career stages of dental practice. As with any business, there will be years of surplus and years of decline, but the typical dentist will easily work through the cycle. When tracked over a ten-year period, it is evident that income hours and average earnings usually increase by 2% to 5%. Most fee guides allow for a modest increase in fees each year, to keep pace with inflation, and if the competency of the dentist is increasing, another 2% to 5% increase is not uncommon.

CHAPTER 21

Analysis of Dental Practice Gross Income

· ·

For years, provincial and national dental organizations have commissioned studies to ascertain what the "typical" Canadian dentist earns. Most experts conclude that the average gross income, as of 2010 was about $850,000 per full-time solo dentist.

Research conducted by ROI Corporation from 2000 to 2010 supports this conclusion. This analysis, involving practices with a minimum of five years in operation, predicted average yearly gross income increases of 3% to 4%. Increasing patient demand, fee guide increases and other variables contribute to these averages. These findings, when projected further (assuming all factors remain more or less the same), suggest the typical Canadian dentist was generating fees of about $1 million in 2012.

These studies also confirm that the typical dentist

retains between 35% and 45% of gross income on an adjusted cash flow basis. "Adjusted" means the various studies do not account for spousal wages (unearned) and non-reoccurring expenses such as major renovations, new equipment additions, extensive continuing education, legal fees and others.

As of 2005, the typical dentist would have retained between $210,000 to $275,000 per year before adjustments, not including income taxes payable. By 2015, this should increase to just over $400,000. By 2020, average adjusted cash flow should be roughly $450,000 to $500,000. When compared to other professions, such as general medicine, accounting and law, dentists are presently earning 10% to 30% more, and this trend will likely continue. With this in mind, it is easy to see that dental practices will remain a popular choice for those seeking to obtain a professional degree!

CHAPTER 22

Suggested Fees
and the Art of Scarcity

. . . .

Dentists are provided with guidelines as to the fees they should charge in almost every province. This is a service provided by dental bodies and associations, and it is a useful tool for determining fees that are fair for both dentists and patients. Fees are highly dependent upon the skill set and the ability of the dentist to communicate the worth of the service to the patient.

If the large majority of dentists charge similar fees regardless of experience, are the fees fair?

This is a sensitive topic particularly when discussed with older, experienced dentists. Many feel the practice of a set fee-guide is unfair as it does not recognize their experience and higher competency. In almost every other business, experience warrants higher fees. Those with greater skill and a wider scope of knowledge charge more than those with less. Lawyers, accountants and even dental specialists are evidence of this practice.

What Fees Are Fair?

The fee guide is ideal for the dentist with less than ten years experience. Those who continually learn new techniques and expand their skills should be charging more than the suggested fees. How much more? Increments of 2% to 3% are not uncommon and several ROI clients consistently charge 5% to 10% above the customary fees charged in their area. One client was charging 30% above the suggested fee for several procedures, including crowns. When informed that he may be the most expensive dentist in the community, he replied:

> *"I should hope so or there's something wrong with my service!"*

This cogent reply concisely explains the belief that skills and ability are necessary to deliver optimum dental care. It might become the basis by which dentists explain their elevated fees.

Practising the Art of Scarcity

As a dental practice grows, confidence and experience allow for increased demands on daily scheduling. Many dentists utilize auxiliaries to help with increased patient flow, such as expanded duty hygienists and level II dental assistants. When the ability to manage patient flow exceeds capacity, the temptation to hire an associate dentist then arises. This is a wonderful opportunity to take the practice into one of two directions:

1. Group practice with two or more dentists
2. The refined solo practice

Group practice has much appeal to those who wish to continue to grow a patient base. The need for treatment can only be addressed by adequate dental manpower. Statistically, the large majority of dentists are unaware that they are actually losing money by employing associates. A well-known study by R.K. House reported that

> *"In most instances, the Principal is actually subsidizing their associate."*

This is true because

- In the first year, principals lose money on associates as they have yet to perfect working within the practice, gain the trust of the patients and increase their competency to "get up to speed."
- In the second year, principals typically break even on associates when they effectively begin to share the patient load.
- In the third year, principals profit from associates.

Here's a fact that most principals neglect to consider:

The average tenure of an associate is less than two years!

The solo dentist with too many patients is very fortunate. The practice can be perfected and controlled, without the need for an associate dentist. Dentists can optimize their time while restricting their availability. This begins with the decision to remain as a solo dentist — the chosen model of over 75% of Canadian dentists. These dentists may reduce their need to increase patient numbers and rely on patients that suit their individual style. Many dentists interviewed relate five main reasons why they chose this model:

- Fewer patient visits per day
- Increased hourly income
- Lower staff turnover
- Higher professional satisfaction
- Less stress

Dentists are taught, from the beginning of their career, to attract new patients and to keep them. This is common for all businesses. However, in most businesses, capacity can be expanded to serve an increasing volume by adding machinery and staff. Dentistry is not compatible with this expansion theory. It is the dentist who must perform the bulk of the income-producing duties as only a limited volume of work can be delegated. When patients' needs exceed the dentist's availability, it's time to reduce the needs, not to increase the dental manpower. Scarcity is the art of being available, but not too accessible. Reducing hours, increasing fees and tightening the collection policies will lead to a reduction of patients to the point that the dentist's schedule is full, but only for the hours he/she wishes to work.

The term "compassion fatigue" was coined by a consultant who studied dental professionals. He found that the desire to be a health care provider often took priority over the desire to be a successful business person. Dentists should be commended for making themselves available for the care of their patients. However, at what point does this obligation become a burden? Dentists are known for giving too much of themselves, often at the expense of their own health. Dentistry has proven to be a high-stress occupation, and it should be remembered that all dentists must seek a balance between career and all other aspects of their lives, especially time with family and friends. When their appointment book is full and an emergency presents a high level of stress because of lack of time, then it is time to reschedule at a slower rate.

One client revealed that he had to work late most nights, rarely took a lunch and had little time for communicating with his patients. He was busy — very busy! He admitted that he did not feel that he was providing adequate care, as he could not enjoy longer appointments to treat his patients and meet their total needs. His year-end figures looked impressive, but there was a cost. He was gaining weight, sleeping poorly and showing many signs of burnout. His solution was to add an associate to relieve him of some of the excess work.

One year later, he had gained more weight and his wife indicated his health was suffering. He confessed that he had too many patients and not enough time to treat them. He believed that the goal of all dentists was to acquire a large patient load. To this end, he was successful, liked by his patients and he received many new referrals.

The young associate he hired was not intending to stay long term and was not particularly adept at handling a busy schedule. The dentist's stress level increased when staff and patients complained of long waits and backlogs. The situation became untenable when the associate moved on to a new opportunity.

The dentist had two choices at this juncture: repeat the process and hire another associate, or drastically cut back his work schedule. He felt selfish when he chose to reduce his hours. He was fearful he would lose the respect of his patients and suffer income loss.

One year later, the dentist had lost weight, appeared less stressed and was happy. What did he do? He raised his fees, reduced his hours and gladly referred those patients who were unhappy to another dentist. In effect, he set a target of fewer patients, not more! He reduced scheduling demands, saw fewer patients per day, and made longer appointments per patient — all resulting in higher fees.

The lesson to be learned is simple. Dentists must care for their own needs first before they can give quality care to others.

CHAPTER 23

Hiring an Associate

. . . .

ROI Corporation has always advocated strongly in favour of the solo practice. However, there are many dentists who at some point will hire an associate. When doing so, plan to do two things:

1. Enter into a written agreement.
2. Plan for the associate's departure.

While there are a few instances of successful, long-lived relationships between dentist and associate, the career associate is rare. Most dentists desire to be their own boss and wish to be so sooner rather than later. They are ambitious, energetic and can bring energy and new ideas to a practice. Rarely are the dentist and the associate in total agreement with regard to the philosophy of the practice.

From a positive perspective, associates can relieve the dentist of an excessive patient load, allow the dentist more time off and extend annual holidays. On the other hand, the associate needs help to learn the trade, gain experience and develop competency. This can only be accomplished if the dentist and associate work closely together. In many instances, this does not happen and the two dentists often find themselves on opposing career paths.

One young associate confessed that her principal was well educated, very competent and had much to offer. In the early stages, they shared caseloads and information and enjoyed an excellent working relationship. After a while, the associate began to feel neglected as the owner took more time away from the office — which was one of his reasons for hiring the associate in the first place. The associate became the predominant caregiver in the practice, assuming more responsibility than was first intended. She felt overworked and even mentioned that she was now responsible for management duties that were not officially delegated nor compensated for.

As she more or less became the lead dentist, the demands grew beyond her ability, given that she had only graduated a few years earlier. The staff began to feel neglected as she would postpone decisions until the principal could be consulted — something that became increasingly difficult to arrange.

The situation worsened when the associate discovered that she was pregnant and had an increasing need for additional time off for health reasons. She did not mention her situation to the principal for fear of being replaced. Then the practice really began to suffer. The staff could not manage all the patients with the decreasing dentist schedule. The dentists were not adequately supervising the office, as neither could devote adequate time to the business, and patients felt they were being unfairly put off for needed care.

The staff finally approached the principal after numerous patient complaints. What was he to do? He enjoyed a luxurious, part-time work schedule and a well-developed personal lifestyle. The office had generated a reasonable profit for over a year, and it afforded him a comfortable income.

With reservations, he decided that it was time to return to full-time practice to catch up on the backlog. In doing so, he reunited with many long-standing patients who began to express their concerns about the lack of attention and delayed appointments. Out of duty to the patients, his schedule then increased rapidly — much faster than he was mentally prepared for. Once again, he found himself in need of an associate, and he questioned the wisdom of repeating his earlier choice to hire one in the first place.

He decided that two part-time associates would be the solution, so as to reduce the risk of having a similar experience. Within six months, he had secured two such associates.

Ironically, the first associate he had hired delivered a healthy baby and asked if she could return to the practice about six months afterwards. Now the principal had three part-time associates, all of whom he felt obligated to keep busy. He then returned to his limited schedule, working only one or two days a week and once again taking several months off, all the time thinking he had regained the ideal schedule.

Then, about one year later, with all three part-time associates showing positive signs, he made the difficult decision to sell the practice and exit dentistry altogether. To his dismay, not one of the part-time associates was interested in buying the practice — they all had other career plans in various stages of development. Sadly, when the principal announced his intentions to sell, each associate accelerated his/her other plans, giving notice of leave one shortly after the other. As tensions grew and each dentist's objectives grew further apart, the practice once again suffered.

After a year-long process, the owner managed to identify a suitable candidate to purchase the office and take over all the management duties.

The post mortem of this transaction reveals that the office sold for less than it was worth, the owner was subjected to several years of rapid change in lifestyle and workload and all the dentists ended up feeling somewhat disappointed that their intentions, while honourable, were never respected by the others.

CHAPTER 24

Upgrading the Facility and Equipment, and the Issue of Overcapitalization

• •

Every practice requires upgrades at some point in its lifespan. In some cases, it may be 10 or 20 years before major equipment needs replacing. Certain items last longer than others, such as dental chairs, stools, x-rays and cabinets, while some need replacing more frequently, such as hand pieces, curing lights, sterilizers, x-ray developers (for traditional film) and computers. When upgrading, resist the temptation to purchase a new technology unless it can prove that it will speed delivery of care, improve patient comfort or increase profitability. The suppliers have extensive training to help the dentist with these decisions.

Upgrading a Facility

What impression does your office leave with your patients? Dental office design and décor have changed dramatically over the past 20 years. Numerous observations reveal that some older offices have outdated and undesirable appearances, while other offices are opulent, fashionable and even extravagant. The key is to strike a balance between the image that is desirable and the investment required to make it so. When deciding, experience suggests a conservative décor so as to prevent patients from assuming that you are charging fees to pay for the extravagant surroundings.

The location, community and profile of your patients have bearing on décor. Whether you're serving a middle-income or a higher-income clientele, it is prudent to be modest! Do not subscribe to the overly flamboyant style of office décor unless it suits your individual personality and you are able to remodel as styles and fashion change.

One practice we appraised had invested over $1.5 million in technology, décor and equipment. It was stunning. Highly regarded patients were asked what their impressions were. They commented that the facility was incredible and they were impressed with their new dentist's commitment. However, when pressed, they wondered if the fees they were paying were above the norm to pay for such facilities. An examination of the dentist's most recent financial statements revealed that the fees charged were actually in keeping with the fee guide for the area. However, the impression of a high-cost practice had already been formed in the patients' minds and they were skeptical. In summary, most dentists should decorate with style and with modesty. The exceptions to this rule are those dentists who have the desire to be seen as the most advanced in the profession.

Overcapitalization

One unfortunate side effect of over-investing in the practice is the theory of diminishing returns. Essentially, this economic principle dictates that dentists will only be able to earn a certain level of fees, regardless of the investment made. Patient flow, the nature of their patients and community demographics dictate that dentists will only be able to generate a certain level of income, no matter how much they have spent on the office.

Years of observation and research suggest that investment in the practice should not exceed an average figure of one year's gross income. An average of the last three years of gross income should be used to calculate this figure. If investment exceeds this amount, then the practice is overcapitalized. New dentists should use the projected average gross income for years five and beyond to determine how much to invest. Only about 30 to 35% of solo dentists grossed over $1 million in 2015. ROI Corporation's findings suggest that many dentists have invested more than is required and are experiencing diminishing returns.

Selling the Opulent Practice

Overcapitalization carried to an extreme creates an opulent office. These ultramodern, high-tech offices are impressive to many of today's young dentists.

When compared to the facilities they trained in at dental school, it is easy to see why.

Upon closer investigation, many young dentists become intimidated by high-tech offices and often say they could never afford to buy such an office. The finance companies also have some resistance to these operations. Even if the cash flow supports the investment, they have serious concerns about the novice dentist's ability to replicate the cash flow to afford the high costs of debt service and maintenance.

While these modern offices remain saleable, it is often at a diminished return to the owner. Due to the reservations of both buyers and their financiers, the offered price is often lower than the reasonable fair market value, if only due to the conservative nature of the cash flow projections they make when investigating a purchase.

Comparatively, the modest office, with total investment of less than one year's average gross, will almost always produce adequate cash flow, even for the young buyer, and financing is obtained in most instances.

While there are always exceptions, the ratio suggested here to determine overall practice investment is a result of long standing observation and analysis.

CHAPTER 25

Continuing Education: Perfecting Clinical and Communication Skills

• •

There are more courses available to the dentist than ever before. One ROI client discovered that the number of lectures available in a year was over 250. Most of these were clinical, but some were of a business nature. The majority of clinical courses focused on aesthetics, implantology and endodontics. The most common business course focused on patient communication skills — for both dentists and their staff. Educators know that dentists lack training in these areas, and they offer a wide array of choices to fill this need.

Clinical continuing education helps dentists to improve their speed of delivery and to provide a wider scope of treatments. However, there are limits to what a dentist can do in any given day. One client had taken so many courses that he became confused as to what he could offer his patients. He had purchased a number of devices that expanded his scope of treatment, but could only find time to use one or two of them regularly. While he was a competent dentist, he was overwhelmed with the options he had learned to offer.

Over time, he became resolved to subspecialize in a few areas beyond traditional restorative treatments, and found himself referring out the usual amount of work. He accidentally became overeducated, to the point where he had difficulty choosing what his core competencies were. It's tempting to study and learn from the experts, however

A wise business owner knows exactly what they do best, and they attempt to perform it often. The wiser business owner knows when to refer work out!

If there is one course of non-clinical study in which the dentist should enroll, it is the art of communicating with patients. All dentists know how to speak in dental terms, but some have great difficulty effectively listening to patient concerns and addressing them.

The typical patient enters a dental office with preconceived notions of dental care, some that were formed many years before today's modern techniques were developed. Many patients have fears and anxieties about visiting a dentist.

Communication is paramount to gaining patients' trust and cooperation in maintaining good dental health. With this thought in mind, all dentists are advised to take courses designed to improve their skills in relating to their patients and minimizing patient fears and uncertainties. In doing so, dentists' case acceptance rate will increase, as will their profits.

LEAVING THE BUSINESS PROFITABLY

CHAPTER 26

The Art of the Appraisal

· ·

The appraisal document is the factual presentation for numerous financial and legal issues. The appraisal defines what the dentist has built for himself/herself and what it is worth in today's market. It is not a management report of suggestions for future growth.

A professional appraiser, with their accreditations, standards and no conflict of interest, will assure the client of quality work and complete confidentiality. Their objectivity ensures that readers of the appraisal (accountants, lawyers, bankers, insurers and potential buyers) can do so with confidence.

The appraisal can be used for many purposes: insurance, estate planning, borrowing of funds or refinancing of existing funds, buying another practice (sometimes they merge together) or a family business transition. All of these purposes need the appraisal statement to document the value of the practice.

The author's philosophy of the appraisal has always been that it is designed, written and formatted for the intended reader. The intended reader is a specific dentist. Lawyers, accountants, bankers, consultants and family members also read appraisals, but the intended reader is the dentist.

Thirty or forty years ago the appraisal was not necessary because dental practices were not worth anything. Why would you pay $1,000 in 1972 to have your practice appraised if it was only going to sell for $5,000?

As the market has developed, the need for appraisal has grown simply because the value of dental practices is getting higher and higher. At the time of publication, practices were selling for a million or two million or more dollars. It is understandable that a bank, a lawyer, an accountant and a purchaser would want a proper appraisal.

Owners are sometimes reluctant to invest in the appraisal because they have a pretty good idea what their business is worth. Their accountant may have given them some advice, or they may have heard about other transactions of classmates; for example, "His business is just like mine so it is probably worth $500,000." A buyer will not accept that.

When people sell their house, the first thing they do is interview two or three real estate agents. A part of that process is not only interviewing them and their marketing plan, but also finding out what the house is worth. In effect, they are getting two or three appraisals before they list the house.

Why would professionals not invest in a proper appraisal so that they know where they stand? This is particularly important if a dentist is thinking of transitioning a practice.

Appraisals have become an absolutely essential planning tool. For the sale of the business, it is mandatory. But it is also becoming a mid-career planning tool. "If my business is worth half a million today, what will it be worth in ten years? Will I be able to retire at 57 or 66 or whatever my retirement plan might be?"

Appraisals are also becoming an elective product that dentists are pursuing in mid- or late-career to explore the question, "What are my options?"

The Process

In our experience, it takes about a month for a professional appraisal firm to prepare an appraisal from start to finish. It is necessary to identify, document and assign value to the various goodwill factors involved in the practice as well as accurately record the details of all major company assets: manufacturer, value, serial number, age, condition and colour.

An appraisal usually remains valid for about one to three years. This depends on major market fluctuations, which are not that common in dentistry. It also depends on whether the business goes through rapid changes such as expanding, bringing on new staff, buying new equipment, taking over the suite next door or moving across the road to buy a whole new building.

Experience dictates that the appraisal should not be free, even though some firms do offer it as part of their sale package. The fee normally charged is about $5,000 for the appraisal and a separate fee for the sale. Appraisal fees are 100% tax deductible. A reputable professional appraisal will save the dentist both time and money since it is far more likely to be accurate and serve as a usable document.

Essentially, the appraisal fee and the sale fee can be likened to how dentists run their businesses. Patients who go to a dentist to have their teeth cleaned do not expect a rebate if they come back a few weeks later for a couple of crowns. These are separate services, even though they are performed at the same office.

Current Users of Appraisals

Years of observation reveal that there are two groups of dentists. There is the 65+ club, which might be referred to as the traditional generation of dentists. Then there is the baby boomer generation. The boomers are the planners and consumers of professional services. They hire investment advisors, appraisers, brokers, accountants and consultants.

The senior generation is a more do-it-yourself generation. Their thinking has been forged by a post-depression belief in frugal self-reliance. They fix their own equipment. They mow their own lawn. They change the oil in their car.

These dentists will do their own appraisals, often at their peril. They are likely to be inaccurate and unacceptable to purchasers. They will try to sell their own practice using a FSBO (For Sale By Owner) sign. This same practice often occurs in real estate markets reflecting the same skepticism about the need for professional help and guidance.

As mentioned, the boomers are far more likely to hire a professional appraiser. They recognize that the appraisal has become a necessary means of doing business. They are prudent, and also recognize that they cannot leave their practice to their family in case of death.

Martin Houser, a lawyer with Harris, Sheaffer & Co. in Toronto, suggests that 50% of Canadian business owners do not have a will. The appraisal *is* the will of the dentist's business. With an appraisal, dentists or their estate can sell the practice.

Seven Uses of Professional Appraisal

Below are a number of uses of an appraisal for a dentist's practice:

1. The appraisal may be reviewed with an accountant or other practice advisors to identify any opportunities for improvement or change.
2. The appraiser can meet with dentists or their advisors to explain his/her methodology and to assist dentists in preparing a "critical path" plan.
3. The appraisal provides an opinion of the full replacement cost of the practice leaseholds and equipment. Dentists may wish to review their office contents insurance to be certain they are not under- or overinsured.

4. The "minus" adjustments portion of an appraisal is found on the calculation of the goodwill page. These are the negative aspects of the practice as purchasers see it. Some of these items can be changed to increase the value of the practice at little or no cost.

5. A copy of the appraisal should be stored with a dentist's other valuable documents when steps 1, 2, 3 and 4 are complete. The dentist should attach a Letter of Direction, which can be prepared as part of the appraisal, that will help in the event of his/her sudden death or disability. A Last Will and Testament should also be included.

6. To increase the practice income, major appraisal companies can recommend companies and individuals that teach fundamental techniques to help dentists achieve this goal.

7. Years of service in the appraisal business generates a national list of accountants, lawyers, bankers, insurance professionals and practice management consultants who can help with the next phase of the dentist's career, whatever it may be.

CHAPTER 27

Selling the Business

Dentists sell their practice for one of three reasons:

1. *Sickness* — The dentist has developed a serious health problem. Many dentists will hang on in the hopes that they will get well and either work part-time or put in a temporary dentist to help them while their health improves. This is understandable but usually a mistake. Approximately 75% of dentists who go on major disability will not come back to work. If they hang on to their business in the interim, that business will suffer. Experience suggests selling the business and taking the necessary steps and time to get well. If full health is restored, the dentist is free to start again with the benefit of hindsight.

2. *Sick and tired* — "That's enough dentistry for me. I've done this for 30 years, I'm moving on."

Sometimes it is after 40 years or even just 20 years, but for some dentists there comes a time when they choose to move on. Many dentists who are tired of full practice go into academia, consulting or part-time dentistry as a non-owner. This can be seen as PTFL (Part-Time For Life) and FFO (Freedom From Ownership). Dentists who choose this route of PTFL and FFO can travel or work in different places. They can work a month and then take a month off as a temporary locum dentist. There are many ways to stay in dentistry without staying chained to a five-days-a-week full-time dental practice and all the responsibilities that come with it.

3. *Financial freedom* — Many dentists have achieved financial freedom because of successful saving and investment plans. Some inherit wealth or have financially successful spouses who make retirement possible. These dentists are the freedom 55 or younger group that can move on from a dental career to do other things.

Numerous reports indicate that roughly 50% of all professionals are between the ages of 50 and 70 as of 2015, and various estimates indicate that approximately 50% of all dentists in Canada are over 55 years of age.

Approximately half of the 22,000 dentists in Canada are now between the ages of 50 and 70. If we extrapolate the exit rate over the next ten years, over 7,500 dentists will exit the profession.

At this point, the projection is that there will *not* be enough buyers to meet the supply of dental practices for sale. The likely result is that prices for practices will fall. This should be evident by 2017.

Today we have more buyers than sellers, particularly in the hotter markets like the Greater Toronto Area, Calgary, Vancouver, and Halifax. Market price is high — the highest it has ever been. It is safe to say that prices for practices have increased dramatically in recent years and were predicted by me to peak somewhere between the years 2014 and 2016 — this has yet to materialize as of late 2016.

Thereafter, there will likely be a slow diminishing of value for dental practices because there are too many dentists selling at once and not enough dentists in line to meet the oversaturation of opportunities.

One possible mitigating factor is a large number of foreign-trained dentists moving to Canada to requalify. They join the third- and fourth-year students at various universities and graduate with the same degree as a traditional dental student.

These dentists are highly motivated, in mid-career and have families. They have mortgages and debts that make them willing to work long and hard hours. Foreign-trained dentists are excellent buyers of dental practices.

These new graduates and foreign-trained dentists should be convinced or encouraged to move to rural Canada. In doing so, their practices would certainly be very lucrative and personally rewarding.

For Sale By Owners
What does a dentist do to sell his/her practice?

Assuming the appraisal is completed, the dentist may or may not then retain the services of a broker.

Although it is becoming less popular, For Sale By Owner (FSBO) still exists. The reason that people try to sell their own practice is to save the commission. However, there is huge risk to selling something on your own — you are unrepresented by a third party.

The main risk is the accidental withholding of information. Both the purchaser and owner do this without even recognizing it. The purchaser is afraid to ask questions, because they do not want to insult the owner. The owner is not certain what to volunteer and many issues go unaddressed.

This accidental withholding of information can turn into negligence that can turn into purposeful misrepresentation, which may end in litigation. Generally speaking, it is all quite innocent yet very costly to the seller.

Both professionals do not want to insult each other. The younger one does not want to insult a senior. A senior does not want to insult a junior because he or she is a potential buyer. Thus, the For Sale By Owner has a very high failure rate.

Dentists, like most of us, are humble, and when they are selling something on their own, they do not want to be seen as too pompous or arrogant or overly confident in themselves or their services. They do not want to appear too aggressive to a buyer. The result is that dentists undersell themselves and their practices.

Dentists accidentally neglect to recognize the strengths of their business as the market sees it.

Unknowingly, they can withhold some of the weaknesses of their business and not expose pertinent information unless asked.

Using a Broker

A broker can explain the weaknesses of a practice and highlight the strengths in ways that an owner cannot. The broker can be more honest (not as modest as an owner) and use the appraisal document to its fullest to support the asking price.

The broker can suggest to late-career dentists how much to improve their practices' environment, equipment and overall appearance before sale. Many dentists often say, "I hear what you are saying. Those are great ideas. I'm tired and I'm ready to sell. Let the next guy do it. If I have to spend an extra $50,000 to sell my practice to earn an extra $100,000 a year later, I would rather sell it today. Let the buyer spend the $50,000 and let them do the work the way they choose. I do not want to live through the renovations."

Experience and many years of observation suggest that this course of action is, in fact, the best. If dentists enhance their practices before selling, they make changes based on what they think is best, rather than what the buyer thinks is best. For example, they may purchase a dental software program that the buyer has found wanting and inadequate. Comments like: "This is the worst dental software program I have ever seen. I am in a practice today that uses it and we do not like it," are common.

Therefore, sellers should not anticipate what

buyers want since they do not know who the buyers are or their preferences. It is better to sell sooner, save the money and effort and let the new owner enhance his/ her new practice in his/her own way.

In preparing a business for sale, dentists should remove all clutter and personal touches (such as family photos and personalized greeting cards). Old equipment is perfectly good if it is working. Some items may need only cleaning, paint touch-ups and other minor cosmetic changes. It is not necessary to spend a lot of money on improvements.

Those who advise a dentist to spend a lot of money just before they sell to increase the "value" of the practice may be doing so out of self-interest. They may have been serving this dentist for 20 or 30 years and want to end the relationship with a lucrative sale.

It really is best to let the buyer make the decisions about upgrades and long-term purchases.

If the owner decides to retain a broker, there are a number of Canadian firms to choose from. Commissions range from a low of 4% up to 10% and by and large reflect the age-old wisdom that "you get what you pay for."

The broker will then advertise the practice and search out potential buyers. Most brokers have a list of "buyers in waiting." In fact, all brokers have the same list because buyers check out each of the brokers. Unlike residential real estate, there are no exclusive "buy only through me" agreements in dental practice sales.

There are no multiple-listing services. Many buyers call all brokers. They have no need to be loyal to any broker. The one that provides them with the best practice in the best location for the right price within their time frame is the broker they will use.

The broker will then start interviewing potential purchasers, qualifying them, and ascertaining their interest and their financial capacity. They will look to see if there is a match between a certain practice and how it is run. They look at location, geography (urban versus rural) and where the buyer's family is located.

There are many reasons someone might be attracted to a certain practice, so brokers try to pre-qualify the buyer as best as possible. A broker will always have the keys and alarm codes to a practice and will selectively and carefully take qualified buyers to see the office. All showings are done after hours. A dental practice is never shown during working hours.

The main reason for this is that the staff should *not* know the practice is for sale. Dentists should never tell staff the business is for sale until the identity of the purchaser is known and the sale is unconditionally final.

To tell staff that the business is for sale, without telling them who is taking it over, often leads to unnecessary fear and uncertainty. They will not know who is taking over and if their jobs are secure.

The time for staff to know that any business has been sold is when the transaction is unconditional; that is, there is no going back for either party. At this point staff should be notified and all obligations as determined by the provincial Employment Standards Acts must be met. Most buyers keep the existing staff because it helps to retain the patients of the purchased practice.

When a buyer has seen the practice after hours — note that the buyer has *not* met the dentist selling the practice as yet — the buyer takes the appraisal to his/her accountant for assessment, then to a banker to see about financing, and then, if the buyer is serious, he/she starts talking to the broker or perhaps to a lawyer about drafting an Offer to Purchase.

From the moment the dentist decides to retain a broker to sell their business to the point where an Offer to Purchase is drafted may take from one month to a year. It depends on the location of the practice, the style of practice (general dentistry versus more expensive cosmetic dentistry) and the overall size of the practice.

There are many factors that can impact the demand for the business. Today, in particular, demographics and geography are the main factors. Many buyers want to be in major urban centres. In major urban practices, the selling process is usually shorter than in rural or remote communities.

As a courtesy by the broker, a draft is often drawn up and then sent to the buyer and his/her circle of advisors for review, discussion and modification. An Offer to Purchase document usually results.

Once an offer has been drafted, the buyer signs it first and his/her deposit (usually 10% of the purchase price) is affixed. The broker delivers it to the seller. The seller is usually given a week to make a decision (consulting with his/her advisors — an accountant and a lawyer). The seller has three options:

1. Accept the offer as is.
2. Reject it outright (which is very rare).
3. Make a counter-offer (which is the most common response).

The counter-offer is simply a message that says: "I accept the bulk of your terms but I would like to change the date or perhaps the price and negotiate some of the conditions." Once mutual agreement is reached, an Accepted Offer of Agreement to Purchase and Sale is prepared.

The agreement then goes through a 10 to 15 day conditional period where the purchaser is allowed to do final inspections of the office, verify that his/her financing is available, and contact the landlord to make sure the premises lease is satisfactory.

If the building is owned by the dentist (which is the case about 30% of the time), it is sold as part of the deal from one dentist to the other and usually requires a property appraisal and a building inspection.

The closing date is 30 to 90 days from the Accepted Offer of Agreement to Purchase and Sale.

Patients are not notified until the closing date and the seller has the buyer's money. Informing patients of the pending sale leads to confusion and uncertainty, especially if something goes awry. It is important to minimize any uncertainty for patients, staff, landlords and suppliers by using a well-thought-out process that a professional broker can provide.

Once the deal is unconditional, the staff are notified of the buyer's intentions. Other things to be done include notifying insurance agents and advisors, and preparing letters to patients about the change of ownership and the closing date.

Seller and Buyer Working Together

Experience suggests that in nine out of ten transactions, the owner should not stay on and associate with the buyer. Some brokers recommend the very opposite and encourage an "after sales" relationship between new and old owners.

Documentation reveals that the seller and buyer are usually from different generations and different cultures, have different training, went to different universities and have different philosophies and different needs.

If the previous owner stays on with the pretense that it will help with patient retention, the buyer now has a dentist working for him/her who cannot change his/her ways. The patients and staff will gravitate to the old dentist out of convenience and habit. Ironically, the buyer still has to pay him/her to be there.

Patients go to a dental practice for many reasons and, as previously mentioned, the dentist is *not* the main reason. This is a sobering fact and the seller must come to understand that anyone is replaceable.

Follow-Up After Sale

Reputable firms act exclusively for the seller. However, it should be remembered that every buyer is a potential client for the firm in 20 or 30 years. To ensure satisfaction, a reputable firm will survey purchasers one year after the sale to learn what has happened with the practice. Two questions should be asked:

1. Did your patient count go up or down?
2. Did your revenue go up or down?

Based on years of surveys, it can be concluded that buyers will retain 85% to 95% of the previous patients. In addition, their own marketing and presence can substantially increase the number of patients overall.

On average, revenue after one year is up 10% to 15%. In some cases, the revenue increase is much higher, usually because of the younger dentist's desire to get out of debt and make the practice profitable as quickly as possible.

Buying a dental practice is a prudent, proven investment, and the vast majority of dentists survive and prosper in the first year. There are many survey examples revealing that dentists have doubled their billings and revenue in one year. There are few investments that rival the purchase of a dental practice by a highly motivated young dentist.

Revenue Growth

The Canadian population is aging and will require more and more dental services. Increasingly, the Canadian population understands the need for dentistry for cosmetic reasons.

The many advances made in cosmetic surgery procedures have caused a remarkable increase in cosmetic dentistry. The baby boomers want to look good and are willing to spend the money on whatever procedures they believe will enhance their overall appearance. This was not the case with previous generations and bodes well in both the long and short term for dental practices.

Five Things You Should Do When Buying a Dental Practice

1. Prospective buyers should call all of the brokers that advertise in *Oral Health Magazine*. Buyers are obligated to contact each broker because brokers do not share their listings with each other like residential real estate agents do. In other words, there's no Multiple Listing Service (MLS) and if you only call one broker, you will not be aware of all the different opportunities available to you.

2. In order to investigate the entire market of practices for sale, dentists should also write or call each of the For Sale By Owner advertisements. These are private sales. They can usually be found in the classified advertisements and they sometimes use a box number at the magazine to screen their inquiries. Unfortunately, it takes a long time to get a reply from a box number, and sometimes you get no reply at all because private sellers receive dozens of letters from all over the world.

3. Find a good accountant. He/she will become the dentist's most trusted source. The accountant will look at all the different financial information the dentist receives while investigating practices. Most accountants charge an upfront fee and/or an annual fee to help you find the right practice. They will also prepare proposals for the bank and help the dentist with personal and business tax planning.

4. It is important to establish a relationship with a financial institution. Chartered banks are willing to review the appraisals dentists have acquired to pre-approve their loan. However, these institutions are often reluctant to go through the entire credit application process until the dentist has shown them an accepted Offer to Purchase.

5. After looking for one to two years, a buyer may identify the "right" practice. At this time it is prudent to see a lawyer and begin discussing your Offer to Purchase. Most brokers will draft an offer for you, at no charge, and will send it to your lawyer. The broker should also process and make the changes your lawyer wants in order to have the final offer ready for signature.

CHAPTER 28

Trends and Predictions

• •

"Change doesn't occur in our lives until the pain of living outweighs the pain of change."
— OMER K. REED, D.D.S.

There are important marketplace trends of which every beginning, mid-career and end-of-career dentist should be aware. The author's predictions are based on decades of research and experience.

Peaks and Valleys
By 2018, the value of dental practices will peak. Then there will be a slow decrease in value for dental practices nationwide.

In rural and remote communities, practices will experience a more rapid decline simply because graduate dentist profiles indicate that they do not want to leave urban centres. This same trend is evident in medical practices today.

Family physicians do not want to go to small rural or remote towns (no matter what incentive plans are put in place). It is not attracting them because their desired lifestyle may be found in the bigger cities. For the most part, economic incentives are not working. Thus, rural and remote practices will experience a decline in value of about 5% to 10% per year between the years 2010 and 2020. This is a most unfortunate development and will have great impact on rural dentists and patients alike.

Deregulation of Ownership Structures

The most apparent trend with regard to regulated professions such as dentistry is toward deregulation. Deregulation is evident with regard to pharmacists, real estate brokers, business brokers, optometrists, legal professionals and many other professionals. All have seen or are going to see less regulation in both ownership structure and owner privileges.

It is highly probable that anyone will be able to buy and run a dental practice as long as licensed dentists perform the dentistry.

Should deregulation occur as predicted, the value of dental practices will temporarily surge and three to five years later, values will drop more rapidly. What this means is that lay people (i.e. non-dentists) can invest and buy dental practices in the same way they can buy a Tim Hortons or McDonald's franchise. Owners do not have to work there — they only have to invest in them and hire staff to run them.

There is an emerging trend in dentistry where investor dentists merge or create a chain of practices. Within a couple years, there will be non-dentist investors who are buying practices and hiring dentists to do the work. They may possibly consolidate practices, bulk up a practice, do multiple purchases or create chains.

Deregulation of the ownership structure exists in many parts of the world including the United States and is coming to Canada. Such a trend may be helpful to young dentists who want to raise their families while also practising dentistry. By working for a practice owned by someone else, they can do their hands-on work without having to deal with the administration of the practice.

As a flood of new buyers enter the dental practice market, the value of these practices will fluctuate. There will be a flurry of purchases, acquisitions and mergers. Then the market will surge and decline, as opposed to the long-term ramp-up that occurred up to now, followed by a long-term diminishing of values in the marketplace. Deregulation has the potential to bring a massive spike followed by a decline in dental practice sales.

These types of new buyers will run out of practices to buy and so there will be fewer buyers in a short time period. There are only so many properties for sale at any time. Regardless of price, many dentists will not sell their businesses and as a result, there will be a quick absorption of the existing supply for sale. The buying frenzy will be over.

There will probably be some decline in values

and then the cycle could repeat itself again starting in 2020 and beyond.

Revenue Explosion
In 2012, the dental industry generated about $14 billion in dental fees for services that the Canadian public consumed — 80% of which is covered by insurance companies and 20% of which is covered privately.

Statistics Canada reported that Canadians spent $9.94 billion in 2007. A reasonable prediction for 2020 is that dentistry revenues will exceed $20 billion.

To a large and ever-increasing extent the revenue increases will be a result of increased cosmetic procedures. The boomer generation will live longer and require more of the aforementioned procedures. This is good news for the revenue side of dentistry.

Female Dentists
Female dentists will be the greatest single demographic that will change the landscape of dental practices for the next two decades. A female dentist will follow a similar career path to a male, with some exceptions:

1. They typically work fewer hours per week because of family, household and personal commitments.
2. They rarely venture outside of the major cites to establish or buy a practice.
3. They work fewer years in full-time practice and exit the profession at younger ages.
4. They gravitate toward part-time associate practices more than males.

Dentistry will continue to attract an ever-increasing number of women in the profession.

Foreign-Trained Dentists

Many of the faculties of dentistry across Canada charge substantially higher tuition fees to dentists who emigrate from other countries to requalify here. Canadian students may pay only 20% to 30% of what a foreign-trained student pays annually (although Canadians must go for four years rather than the two years required of foreign dentists).

It makes economic sense to open more positions for foreign-trained dentists to come to Canada to requalify. Dental faculties can expand class sizes to accommodate these changes or they can allocate more positions to foreign-trained dentists, thereby reducing the number of spots available to Canadian-born-and-raised applicants.

If dental faculties expanded the number of graduates in the coming ten years (both domestic and foreign trained), there would be an increase in the number of buyers in the marketplace. More buyers increases the value of dental practices the boomer generation dentists will be selling, while also providing more and more Canadians with their own dentist.

Tim's Tips

. . . .

1. An astounding number of business owners do not have a will. At a recent conference in Waterloo, only 18 of 40 dentists polled had a current version of a legal will. It is widely acknowledged that more than 65% of business owners are will-less. Not only does this lack foresight with regard to your benefactors, it is a *colossal* oversight on behalf of your business. Get a will!

2. If you suffer a serious illness, take the necessary time and actions to rectify this development. If necessary, sell your practice. Experience has shown that it rarely pays to try to keep the business going in a haphazard way or to use an associate to get you through the rough times. Should your health be completely restored and you so desire, start again with the benefit of hindsight. You have only one life! Enjoy the fruits of your labour.

3. If a short-term illness or disability occurs, it is wise to have a locum dentist in your employ who can temporarily take over and carry the practice. Locums are becoming an ever increasing and popular way to deal with short-term illness or patient overflow.

4. Be aware of compassion fatigue and practise the art of scarcity when determining the hours worked and stress endured. Seek a balance between work and play. Be aware of burnout and realize that you can provide quality care only when your own personal needs have been met.

5. When selling a practice, never reveal your plans to staff or patients until the sale has been completed unconditionally.

6. The vast majority of graduating dentists will prefer to locate in major Canadian cities. To date, no amount of incentives, by government and otherwise, has been sufficient to change this trend. However, it disregards the fact that there are a number of lucrative, creative and personally rewarding practices available in many non-urban centres across the country. It is believed that rural dentists have averaged gross income of well over a million dollars a year. Their overheads will be substantially lower.

7. The most successful form of dental practice is the solo dental practice. At least 75% of all practices fall into this category.

8. Young dentists seeking a dental practice to purchase must be cautious and patient. Finding the right practice for you takes time. Usually, the right practice will present itself to you. The right practice is one in which the clinical procedures and overall operation mirrors the purchaser's dental philosophy.

9. Most graduating dentists are not ready to buy an existing practice or establish a new practice of their own for at least three to five years. These new graduates often find success as an associate dentist in that interval.

10. Dentists opening a new dental office in a plaza setting in a major city are likely to experience two years of expenses exceeding income. It is prudent to have sufficient financing in place so that this anticipated initial negative cash flow can be met.

11. The referrals you receive from your patients of their friends, family and acquaintances are crucial. Ultimately, it is the most important factor in growing a new dental practice. It pays to treat your patients well!

12. Be careful about discounting your fees for dental services. Once this practice becomes common knowledge, it is difficult in the future to charge what your service is truly worth.

13. Solo dentists should look for an office of approximately 1000 to 1200 square feet. This size is optimal from the perspective of need, comfort and economy.

14. The dental office should be ergonomic and elegant in its simplicity, both in terms of its design and function.

15. Dentists should sit in their operating chairs regularly in order to see and feel what their patients experience. Often this leads to improvements in both service and office presentation.

16. The most important aspect of buying an existing practice is the patient list. In essence, this is the "business" you are buying. Elementary research can reveal much about this list, including the overall number of patients, as well as their gender, age, ethnicity and insurance coverage. Know what you are buying.

17. The face of dentistry is changing as more and more women enter into dental practice. In addition, more and more foreign-trained dentists will be an integral part of the Canadian dental profession.

18. Dentists should work in their areas of expertise and specialty and know when to refer other work to other dentists.

19. Cosmetic dentistry, especially as demanded by the so-called "boomer generation," will become the most lucrative part of most dental practices. Basic cosmetic procedures should become the structure upon which a practice is built.

20. The total investment in a dental practice should *not* exceed the average of three years' gross income. Any further investment results in a diminishing return on investment.

21. It is evident that investment in dental practice ownership will extend to non-dentists because of deregulation. Corporate-style dental chains will continue to emerge and become a significant part of dental practice.

22. Refrain from office romances. Maintain a friendly but professional relationship with all employees.

23. Communicate with your staff. Praise them for work well done. Gently remind them when they are not meeting your expectations and move on. Compensation should be based on industry standards, seniority and, most importantly, on quality of work.

24. All dentists should have a well-defined office policy manual. It should clearly define expectations between dentist and staff as well as inter-staff expectations. From time to time this manual should be revised and staff informed of any changes.

25. When considering the sale of your dental practice, it is essential that you employ the services of a dental practice sales firm. When it comes to selling their practice by themselves, dentists often underestimate and undersell their practices. Sometimes, quite innocently, they withhold critical information about their practice in terms of both its strengths and weaknesses. Hire a professional!

26. Many dentists state that they should have retired earlier. Know that there can be a meaningful and rewarding life after dentistry.

Appendix A: Curriculum Vitae for Timothy A. Brown

www.roicorp.com
www.profitable-practice.com

Chief Executive Officer, ROI Corporation

Dental, Veterinary and Optometry practice appraisal, brokerage, financing, Associate and Locum placement and practice management consulting.

- Began working for family-owned business in 1979, at the age of 16.
- Broker of Record and Appraiser responsible for the opinion of fair market value for all professional practices evaluated by the firm — nationwide.
- Author of *Profitable Practice: Why a Dental Practice is an Exceptional Investment*, now in 7th printing with over 6,000 copies in distribution.
- Publisher of *Profitable Practice Magazines* — Dental, Veterinary & Optometry
- Established *Locum Lifestyle*™ the concept promoting dentists (Locum Tenens) who work in part-time, temporary assignments.
- Created *EthicLease* an equipment finance company.
- Conceptualized and trademarked *Investor Dentist*™ and *i-Dentist*™ the growing market of third party buyers investing in Canadian dental practices.
- Conceptualized and trademarked *Investor Vet*™ and

i-Vet™ the growing market of third party buyers investing in Canadian veterinary practices.

- Recognized industry expert & keynote speaker at hundreds of Continuing Dental Education seminars including: Canadian Dental Association, Ontario Dental Association, Alberta Dental Specialists, International Dental Congress, Dental Society meetings, Study Clubs, Canadian Dental Faculties and Dental Alumni Associations.
- Author of 250+ articles published in private publications and dental journals.

Previous Career History:

- 1989-1990; specialized in financing for dental practice purchases.
- 1987-1988; worked directly with Dr. Howard Rocket to negotiate the sale of franchised dental practices with Tridont Dental Centers.

Education:

1997 to 2015 – 360 hours of Mandatory Continuing Education

1996 – Professional Real Estate Brokerage, OREA

1996 – Certificate programme, OREA

1995 – I.C. & I., Law, Mortgage Finance, OREA

1990 – Professional Selling Skills III (Xerox)

1989 – Dale Carnegie Sales programme

1987 – Marketing Diploma, Sir Sandford Fleming College

1985 – Principles of Appraisal, Sheridan College

1984 – Real Estate as a Professional Career, Sheridan College

His book *Profitable Practice — Why a Dental Practice Is an Exceptional Investment* is a potent reminder that dentistry can indeed be very profitable if the right steps are taken from the very beginning. Timothy brings these credentials to the podium and delivers a message that inspires and energizes dentists to reach their highest potential. He communicates clearly and concisely, empowering dentists to acquire the business acumen needed for success with his enthusiastic, insightful presentation.

Appendix B: Agreement to Associate

AGREEMENT TO ASSOCIATE

Between

Dr.
(hereinafter referred to as "Owner")

- and -

Dr.
(hereinafter referred to as "Associate")

INDEX

THE ASSOCIATE AGREES: **Page 4**

GENERAL: **Page 6**

AGREEMENT TO ASSOCIATE

THIS AGREEMENT, made in duplicate this ＿＿ day of ＿＿＿＿＿＿＿＿, 2012.

BETWEEN   Dr.   of the City of   , Doctor of Dental Surgery, hereinafter called the
"OWNER" of the First Part,

- AND -

Dr.   of the City of   , Doctor of Dental Surgery, hereinafter called the
"ASSOCIATE" of the Second Part.

BOTH PARTIES - THE OWNER AND ASSOCIATE AGREE:

B - 1   That this Agreement is made in good faith and strict confidentiality by the parties hereto
and with mutual trust and confidence in each other.

B - 2   That each party hereto affirms that they acknowledge and subscribe to the Code of Ethics
of the Canadian Dental Association and the rules and regulations prescribed by the
Provincial regulatory body as the guide to their professional conduct in all relations with the
other party, with other dentists and with patients.

B - 3   That for the duration of this contract, they shall carry on the practice of dentistry in all its
branches, devoting their time, ability and energy, without at the same time, neglecting their
duties to the dental profession or their social obligations as citizens and members of the
community.

B - 4   That the duration of this Agreement shall be for a term of   **(   ) years/months**
commencing   provided, however, that in the event that the parties continue in
association with each other after the above period, without entering into a new Agreement
in writing, then all the terms and conditions of this Agreement shall continue in full force
and effect during the said period until a new agreement is concluded between the parties.
Provided, however, that either party may terminate the Agreement, during such extended
period, on giving ninety days written notice of termination to the other party.

B - 5   That all business, relating to the aforesaid practice of dentistry, shall be done in the name
of the Owner and all fees and amounts received shall be the property of the Owner. Any
and all cheques made payable to the Associate will be endorsed by the Associate to the
Owner.

B - 6   That all of the patients' charts, x-rays, models, records of names, addresses and telephone
numbers are the property of the Owner (excluding the family of the Associate).

B - 7   That each will be responsible for and pay for their own separate expenses: i.e., licenses,
dues, fees, continuing education, seminars, conventions, personal insurance including
malpractice, auto expenses, gowns and cleaning of gowns.

BOTH PARTIES - THE OWNER AND ASSOCIATE AGREE - Continued

B - 8   That both parties are practising as separate, independent practitioners, each responsible for their own dentistry, licenses, personal finances (including income taxes), accounting costs and legal fees, and further, that this is not an agreement for partnership.

B - 9   That the intent of this Agreement is to set out the main points; to subscribe to fair treatment of each party so that neither will gain at the other's expense, and further that each agree that a sense of community is necessary; i.e. each person feeling a sense of belonging in the organization and closeness with the people, concern and cooperation; individuals ask for and offer each other help, exchanges of constructive criticism and praise, and identify with the office's success and failure.

_____	_____
Initials	Initials

THE OWNER AGREES:

0 - 1   To remunerate and pay the Associate for dentistry rendered, charged and collected by the Associate the sum of   **(**   %**)** after laboratory costs have been deducted.

EXAMPLE:		_$
Gross fees collected from patient		110.00
Less laboratory fees		10.00
Balance to be divided		100.00
Practice overhead	60%	60.00
Associate receives	%	____

0 - 2   To pay the Associate a flat rate fee of   dollars ($) for recall examinations the Associate performs. All other fees charged or earned by the Hygienist will be credited to the Owner.

0 - 3   To provide and pay for the following usual and customary services and operating costs and expenses of the owners practice, not to include the expenses described in paragraph A - 1:

        Accounting and bookkeeping
        Answering services
        Business taxes
        Dental and drug supplies
        Insurance (all risk, office overhead, and liability)
        Janitor (interior cleaning)
        Laundry and cleaning
        Leased equipment
        Advertising
        Bank charges
        Interest (bank)
        Depreciation, Maintenance and repairs
        Office supplies and stationery
        Postage and deliveries
        Rent (occupancy costs)
        Telephone (except Associate's personal long distance)
        Legal, management and consulting fees for the practice
        Wages, salaries, bonus & benefits (including Hygienist)

I

0 - 4   To provide the services of the following staff to the Associate during the agreed practice hours: Chairside Assistant

0 - 5   To pay the Associate in full, monthly on collected amounts, less agreed upon deductions with a statement of fees charged and collected, and further, such payments to be made within seven (7) days following the end of the month, with a draw halfway through each month for the estimated collections to date.

0 - 6   To provide the Associate with his name on the door to the suite or office and other locations, if allowed by the landlord and the regulations of the College.

0 - 7   That the Associate's name will be placed in the telephone book, by the owner, at the owner's expense, and stationery will be supplied provided the Agreement is for two years or longer.

0 - 8   That the Associate may choose the laboratory of his choice for their own laboratory work.

                                                            _____   _____
                                                            Initials   Initials

THE ASSOCIATE AGREES:

A - 1   To be current and pay for his own licenses, dues, fees, continuing education, seminars, conventions, personal insurance including malpractice, auto expenses, gowns, and personal long distance telephone calls.

A - 2   To charge fees for dental treatment and services rendered in keeping with the practice, and to abide by the policies and terms of the practice.

A - 3   To work the days that are mutually agreed upon which are in the best interest of the practice and needs of the community or patients serviced, and specifically the approximate schedule:

Monday..................from   am to   pm

Weekly - ....   days per week (hours at Chairside)
Annually - ....   weeks per year.

A - 4   To notify the Owner one (1) month in advance of any vacation periods desired, and that the Owner will have the first choice should there be any conflict in time desired, to ensure that one practitioner will be in attendance to service the practice.

A - 5   That all patients' records, charts, x-rays and models, including names, addresses and telephone numbers will not be removed at any time, in any manner or way, without the Owner's written permission.

A - 6   That they will not practise at another location within   (   ) miles of this practice during this agreement and for   (   ) years after the termination of this agreement; however, this does not prevent the Associate from practising outside the area as stipulated above during this Agreement to Associate.

A - 7   To not solicit, invite, encourage in any manner whatsoever, any patients known by them to be a patient of this practice, to seek treatment elsewhere or to solicit any employees of this practice to work elsewhere.

A - 8   That it is understood that the Associate will be required to treat emergency and transient patients in the normal course of dental practice and to share after hours calls.

A - 9   To supervise the Hygienist in the absence of the Owner.

A - 10   That all purchases over $200.00 for supplies, drugs, instruments and equipment to be confirmed with the Owner prior to ordering.

A - 11   That supplies, drugs, instruments and equipment which the Associate desires as a personal choice (materials not essential to practise dentistry) will be ordered, billed to and paid for by the Associate. These materials will remain the property of the Associate and a list with invoices will be retained for administration purposes.

A - 12   To conduct their practise of dentistry in the present or agreed to general policies and methods of the office; the clinical and administrative systems including fees charged, payments, credit terms and collection and to record recall examination fees he/she rendered in the Hygienist operatories on the Associate's daily log.

ASSOCIATE AGREES - Continued

A - 13   To be responsible for filing income tax returns and paying his/her own income tax and Canada Pension according to the requirements of Revenue Canada.

A - 14   To put forth the effort to obtain new patients in conjunction with the Owner, including referrals in order to build the practice.

A - 15   To attend and contribute to regular staff meetings held for purposes of practice management, staff coordination and general communications between Owner, Associate and staff.

A - 16   That they will not disclose any information relating to the private or confidential affairs of the Owner during the term of this agreement and at any time thereafter.

_____   _____
Initials   Initials

GENERAL:

G - 1 In the event of the death or incapacity of the Owner, this Agreement shall remain in full force and effect until expiration of this Agreement, unless released at an earlier date by the estate. The Associate would assist the estate in selling the practice and would help maintain the practice until the practice is sold by the estate.

G - 2 In the event of the death or incapacity of the Associate, this Agreement shall be deemed to be terminated as of the date of such death or incapacity, and the terms of this Agreement shall be null and void and at an end.

G - 3 In the event of the sale of the practice by the Owner, this Agreement shall be terminated as of thirty (30) days from the date of closing of the sale transaction and the terms of this Agreement shall be null and void and at an end except the restrictive covenant in paragraph A - 6 which will remain in force until it has been fulfilled.

G - 4 The parties, by entering into this Agreement, enter into an association and not a partnership or an Agreement of Employment, and nothing contained herein or otherwise arising shall constitute the parties as partners with one another, nor shall anything contained herein or otherwise arising constitute the parties as agents for each other.

G - 5 On termination, other than by reason of death or incapacity, the Associate will endeavour to complete all major cases which they have started.

G - 6 In the event of any dispute over the terms of the Agreement, the parties would endeavour to choose a mutually acceptable third party to act as an arbitrator. In the event that the parties are unable to agree as to the choice of arbitrator, then each party would choose one arbitrator and the two arbitrators would choose the third arbitrator. The decision of the majority of arbitrators would govern. The arbitrators would be empowered to resolve any dispute with respect to the interpretation of this Agreement. The expenses incurred by the arbitrators would be shared by the parties. The decision of the arbitrators shall be final and binding with no appeal. The arbitration shall be held within 30 days of one of the parties notifying the other of his/her desire for arbitration.

G - 7 This Agreement will be binding upon the heirs and executors of both parties.

IN WITNESS WHEREOF the parties hereto have hereunder set their respective hands and seals.

SIGNED, SEALED AND DELIVERED
In the presence of:

      }
      }
      }

_____   _____   _____
Witness   Signature of Dr.   (Owner)   Date

      }
      }
      }

_____   _____   _____
Witness   Signature of Dr.   (Associate)   Date

PRACTICE TRANSITION MANUAL

CONGRATULATIONS

On the Sale of Your Practice

It has been our pleasure to work with you to this end.

ROI CORPORATION IS 100% PRIVATELY OWNED AND HAS OPERATED IN CANADA SINCE 1974.

1155 Indian Road, Mississauga, Ontario L5H 1R8 Tel: (905) 278-4145 Fax:(905) 278-4705
www.roicorp.com

ROI Corporation Vendor Transition Manual ©

VENDOR'S ACTIVITIES FOR CLOSING

(After all conditions have been met)

1) **Assignment of Premise Lease**

✓ Request Assignment of your Lease, or written consent to the assignment, from your landlord. (Your lawyer usually arranges this.)

2) **Meeting with New Owner**

✓ Discuss Letter of Introduction & staff policies, scheduling etc.

3) **Staff Notices**
DO NOT deliver notices until the Purchaser has removed ALL conditions.

✓ Arrange staff meeting to announce sale of practice. Prepare "Records of Employment" as of closing. **Records of Employment should be ordered within 3 weeks of closing as they are mailed from the Government of Canada.**

4) **Meeting with the Staff**

✓ Schedule a meeting with the staff to introduce the new owner.

5) **Letter of Introduction**

✓ Printing (photocopying).
✓ Typing envelopes, labels or mail merge.

6) **Accountant**

✓ Advise your accountant of the allocations of the purchase price.

7) **Telephone**

✓ Advise telephone provider of change of ownership. They will send forms for signature.

8) **Insurance**

✓ Advise Insurance Company of cancellation of appropriate policies (effective after closing date). Purchaser <u>may</u> assume existing policy.

9) **Rental Agreements**

✓ Advise companies of cancellation or transfer (if applicable) of any rental agreements. Purchaser <u>may</u> assume leases.

10) **Suppliers**

✓ Do not advise suppliers until the day of closing.

Note: Once the Vendor and Purchaser have agreed on the wording in the introductory letter to the patients (which the Purchaser is responsible to mail as per the agreement), this letter, or any contact with the Vendor's patients by the Purchaser, should not be made until the sale has closed. This is to avoid any possible confusion or damage to the Vendor's practice in the very unlikely event that the sale does not close on time. The Vendor may agree to address and post a few envelopes in advance for those patients with appointments immediately following the close of sale.

PURCHASER'S ACTIVITIES FOR CLOSING

(After all conditions have been met and approximately one month before closing)

1. **Meeting with Vendor**
   - ✓ Draft the Letter of Introduction with Vendors input.
   - ✓ Discuss staff policies, scheduling, mailing (envelopes, stamps, labelling, etc.)

2. **Schedule a meeting with staff (Vendor is to set the date)**
   - ✓ Discuss offers of employment (terms, etc.) after all the conditions are removed on the Offer.
   - ✓ Take a photo of both dentists together in the practice.

3. **Rentals (assume/transfer)**
   - ✓ Rent (security deposit), etc.
   - ✓ Nitrous tanks, etc.
   - ✓ Computer software update.
   - ✓ Debit / Credit card machines (call your bank).

4. **Telephone**
   - ✓ Provide telephone provider with your information after Vendor has notified them of transfer.

5. **Insurance**
   - ✓ Life, disability & fire, etc. effective date of closing.

6. **X-ray Inspection (HARP)**
   - ✓ Advise them of change of ownership.

7. **G. S. T./H. S. T.**
   - ✓ Not applicable on a share sale transaction.

8. **Letter of Introduction**
   - ✓ Postage & mailing of letters on closing.

9. **Reception**
   - ✓ Plan a social function for departing dentist – invite patients.

10. **Stationery**
    - ✓ Personalized letterhead, envelopes, appointment cards, business cards, patient receipts, thank-you notes.

11. **Lawyer's Fees**
    - ✓ Searches, closing documents, registration.

12. **Accountant**
    - ✓ Submit applicable taxes by 15th of following month of close (or as Accountant advises).

13. **Employer Number**
    - ✓ Go to: www.cra-arc.gc.ca/tx/bsnss/menu-eng.html and register for payroll deductions.

14. **Advise suppliers**
    - ✓ Only **after** sale closes and keys in your possession.

ROI Corporation Vendor Transition Manual ©

PRACTICE PURCHASE

NEW OWNER'S STRATEGY

It is important to be aware of the patient's position on the sale of the practice. When a patient is coming to see a new dentist, it is usually because they have selected a dentist of their choice. In a practice transfer situation, the patient was offered no choice. Accordingly, they will be more observant and possibly more critical than if they had handpicked you.

Understanding this profile leads to two common sense rules for the new owner for at least the first visit:

1. Keep things the way they are as much as possible at first. The fewer the changes, the less the patient will have to absorb during their initial meeting with you. The more they can concentrate on you, the sooner they will satisfy their anxiety.

2. A step further than your Code of Ethics is to allow the patients to continue to believe that their previous dentist was competent. Remember, that it was their choice to have that dentist. Any indications that you are a "better" dentist may create a negative thought that the previous dentist was "not so good". This may be perceived to be a challenge to their judgement. For example: A sudden need for extensive dentistry may imply neglect on the part of the previous dentist. It may be more prudent to say that it appears the previous dentist was keeping this under observation but it now appears it is time to consider active treatment to head off any complications.

Any change in treatment and office procedures is more easily accepted if it is a result of some outside force, i.e. new fee guide, recent technology. Changes should be gradual and preferably after second or third visits.

Patient retention, on average, is about 85% – 95% after a sale. You can improve that percentage by taking the above two points into consideration.

These strategies have been compiled after reviewing the comments of hundreds of new owners we have worked with since 1974. This historical perspective is provided to you to minimize patient loss and maximize patient retention.

Here's To Good Dental Health To You And Your Patients!

P.S. Renovations: It might be an idea to advise patients by newsletter of major changes and gently note that these changes will not result in any change of procedures/staff, but are a long term investment in their dental care and comfort.

LETTER OF INTRODUCTION

Standard Wording

Stationery of Dr. _____ (Vendor)

Dear Patients -or- To My Patients:

I have had the pleasure of attending to your dental care for the past many years. Therefore, it is with mixed feelings that I have decided to:

- ❏ relocate closer to my home
- ❏ pursue other interests
- ❏ retire from dentistry
- ❏ retire for the betterment of my health
- ❏ slow down my dental career
- ❏ I want to personally thank you for your trust and confidence in me for the care of your dental needs.
- ❏ I want to personally thank you for permitting me the privilege of caring for your dental needs.
- ❏ I would like to extend my sincere appreciation to all of you.

I am pleased to announce that Dr. _____ D.D.S., will continue your dental care and will provide you with the same professional excellence that I have strived for.

Dr. _____ is a 19/20____ graduate of the University of, Faculty of Dentistry. Since graduation he/she has
_____

I am confident that you will find him/her to be a congenial and capable person.

- ❏ professional and personable
- ❏ is a highly regarded dentist
- ❏ having practised in _____ for _____ years.

We are
- ~ personally acquainted
- ~ have enjoyed a rewarding relationship both as a friend and colleague for some time.

All of your dental records will stay with the practice and the office telephone number will remain the same or will change to _____.

Ms. _____ will be continuing in the office to assist Dr. _____. She will be happy to receive your calls as usual and will ensure that your regular examination and recall appointments are maintained.

I know that I am leaving my patients and my practice in good hands and extend my very best wishes for your health and happiness.

Yours sincerely,

_____, D.D.S.

PRACTICE TRANSITION

When the Previous Owner is NOT With Practice or Unavailable

Suggestions of what to say to patients

Answer Telephone:

Initially, as **"Dental Office"** because the patient will expect to hear the **PREVIOUS** name, not the **NEW** owner's which may confuse them.

Explanation:

Dr._____ has retired, returned to school, or_____(other) and Dr._____ is the new Dentist.

The letter from Dr._____ announcing his retirement or ____(other) and introducing Dr. _____ to you, may not have reached you.

I believe you will find Dr. _____ both capable and considerate of your Dental Health.

All of your dental records, charts and x-rays are here. I would be pleased to arrange an appointment for you.

Dr. _____'s assistant (name) or/and receptionist (name) also our hygienist (name) has remained with the practice.

DENTAL RECORDS

When a practice is sold, the RCDSO Advisory on Change of Practice Ownership _recommends_ the following protocol:

➢ The dentist leaving the practice should notify his or her patients in writing of the change in practice ownership, or pending retirement, and inform them where their dental records can be found.

This excerpt can be found on the Royal College of Dental Surgeons of Ontario website: www.rcdso.org. professional practice/practice advisories. Other provincial regulators _may_ have similar recommendations.

ROI Corporation Vendor Transition Manual ©

Suggested script to announce the sale of a dental practice to <u>Staff</u>:

We suggest that you schedule a staff meeting at the end of a short or light day of practice, and ideally when all staff can be present.

I have been very fortunate to have each of you to support this practice. I know that many of our patients comment about our team approach and how much they enjoy receiving their dental care from all of us.

Therefore, it is with mixed emotions that I have decided to A) Sell my practice and retire – or – B) Reduce my working hours and take more time for myself and my family (i.e. hobbies/travel?).

As you may already know, I have been searching for the ideal candidate to take over the patient load, and I want you to know that I was not certain who this individual would be until very recently. You may have heard some rumors, and I admit that some of them may have been true, <u>to some extent</u>, although I could not notify you until I was sure the 'right' dentist had been secured.

I have asked my chosen successor, Dr. _____ to introduce him/herself to you A) in a few moments – or – B) tonight/tomorrow. *(We recommended that the purchaser be introduced **within 24 hours** of this meeting).*

I have gotten to know him/her over the past few months and know that you will find him/her to be a wonderful, warm & caring dentist who will need your support moving forwards.

I will (will not) continue to work at the practice (If yes, mention the reduced schedule) and I will be available to help all of you, and the patients with this transition. I should also mention that I hired a professional firm who specializes in exactly this process, and the President, Timothy A. Brown has suggested I give you a copy of a column he wrote specifically about his company's experiences in these planned transitions.

If purchaser is to be introduced at this time: "I'm sure that you have questions, and I want to personally address each of them. But before we do that, I would like to introduce Dr. _____ to you – I think you'll really enjoy working with him/her!

This is a suggested script only – circumstances vary – contact your ROI Associate for more advice on this very important step in the process.

EMPLOYMENT STANDARDS INFORMATION

For more information on the Employment Standards Act in your Province please contact your local branch office.

You can also receive information off the Internet at the following websites:

Alberta Employment Standards: http://employment.alberta.ca/SFW/1224.html
Record of Employment forms: 1- 800-561-3992

B.C. Ministry of Labour Employment Standards Branch: www.labour.gov.bc.ca/esb/
Record of Employment forms: 1-888-557-7111

Manitoba Employment Standards Division: www.gov.mb.ca./labour/standards
Record of Employment forms: 1-800-663-0983

Nova Scotia Labour Standards: www.gov.ns.ca/lwd/employmentrights/
Record of Employment forms: 1-800-268-6567

Ontario Ministry of Labour: http://www.labour.gov.on.ca/english/es/
Record of Employment forms: 1-800-263-8364

Quebec Labour Standards: www.cnt.gouv.qc.ca/en/home/index.html
Record of Employment forms: 1-866-368-0372

ROI Corporation Vendor Transition Manual ©

ARTICLES OF INTEREST TO THE VENDOR

SELLING YOUR PRACTICE

http://roicorp.com/selling-a-practice-part-ii/

LETTERS OF INTRODUCTION WHEN SELLING A PRACTICE

http://roicorp.com/letters-of-introduction-when-selling-a-practice/

STAFF ISSUES WHEN BUYING OR SELLING A PRACTICE

http://roicorp.com/staff-issues-when-buying-or-selling-a-practice/

THE LOCUM LIFESTYLE

http://roicorp.com/the-locum-lifestyle/

http://roicorp.com/can-you-afford-to-take-a-break/

Appendix D: Locum Agreement

THIS AGREEMENT made in duplicate this _____ day of _____, 201__

BETWEEN: Dr. _____ of the City of _____, the **"OWNER"**

- AND -

Dr. _____ of the City of _____, the **"LOCUM"**

BOTH PARTIES - THE OWNER AND LOCUM AGREE:

1. That this Agreement is made in good faith and strict confidentiality and with mutual trust and confidence.

2. That each party affirms that he/she subscribes to the Code of Ethics of the Canadian Dental Association and the rules and regulations prescribed by the Provincial regulatory body as the guide to his/her professional conduct in all relations with the other party, with other dentists and with patients.

3. That either party may terminate this agreement on giving twenty (20) days written notice.

4. That all fees charged, and accounts for professional services, shall be rendered in the name of the Owner. All amounts received shall be payable to and be the property of the Owner. Any cheques made payable to the Associate will be endorsed to the Owner.

THE OWNER AGREES:

5. To remunerate and pay the Locum _____ % of the fees charged and collected by the office for dental services the Locum performs after laboratory costs have been deducted. **OR**, to remunerate the LOCUM a daily rate of $_____ for each day worked, not to exceed ____ hours operatory time per day. **OR,** to pay an hourly rate of $_____ for each hour worked. Days and hours worked to be mutually agreed upon.

6. To remit payment to the Locum, in full, less agreed upon deductions, within ten (10) days of statement.

THE LOCUM AGREES:

7. To charge fees as suggested by the Owner and to abide by the policies of the practice.

8. That patients' records, charts, x-rays and models, including names, addresses and telephone numbers, will not be removed at any time, in any manner or way, without the Owner's written permission.

9. That he/she will not solicit any employees or patients of this practice to see work or treatment elsewhere.

10. That he/she will support the continuation of the practice during the sale, or the absence of the owner.

IN WITNESS WHEREOF the parties hereto have hereunder set their respective hands and seals.

SIGNED, SEALED AND DELIVERED, in the presence of:

}
}
}
}

_____   }   _____ Date _____
Witness   Owner

}
}
}
}

_____   }   _____ Date _____
Witness   Locum

Appendix E: Offer to Purchase

OFFER TO PURCHASE SHARES – EXISTING PC
(For Use in the Province of Ontario)

This Offer to Purchase Shares (the "**Offer**") dated this _____ day of _____, 20____.

Between

Dr. _____ (the "**Vendor**")

and

Dr. _____ (the

"**Purchaser**") agrees to purchase all of the shares (the "**Purchased Shares**") of

_____ (the "**Corporation**") currently being carried on by the Vendor (the

"**Practice**"), located at:

_____ (the "**Premises**")

subject to the terms and conditions contained herein for the

PURCHASE PRICE of:

_____ **Canadian Dollars** .... ($_____.00)

(the "**Purchase Price**")

DEPOSIT: The Purchaser submits upon Acceptance of this Offer:

_____ **Canadian Dollars** .... ($_____.00)

by bank draft or certified cheque to ROI Corporation, Brokerage (the "**Brokerage**"), as a deposit (the "**Deposit**") to be held in trust pending completion or other termination of this Offer and to be credited toward the Purchase Price payable on closing, and to further pay the balance of the Purchase Price, subject to adjustment as set out below, by bank draft, certified cheque or electronic money transfer on the Completion Date as stated herein. For the purposes of this Offer as noted above, upon "**Acceptance**" shall mean that the Purchaser is required to deliver the Deposit to the Brokerage within two (2) business days (excluding Saturdays, Sundays and any Statutory Holiday in the Province where the practice is located) following the Acceptance of this Offer. The Parties to this Offer acknowledge that the Brokerage shall place the Deposit in an interest bearing account when the Completion Date noted herein is scheduled for greater than thirty-five (35) days from the execution of this Offer by both Parties. Interest accrued on the Deposit amount, calculated roughly at the financial institution's current rate of prime minus 2.00%, and will be paid to the Purchaser following the successful completion of this transaction. The Purchaser acknowledges the responsibility of disclosing such earnings for tax purposes as deemed necessary.

The parties agree to make a best efforts basis one week before the Completion Date to estimate the working capital of the Corporation (being defined as the cash, and prepaid expenses of the Corporation less the liabilities of the Corporation as determined according to generally accepted accounting principles) as at the Completion Date. In the event that the estimated working capital is a negative amount, the Purchase Price payable on closing will be reduced on a dollar for dollar basis equal to such deficiency (subject to final adjustment according to Section 7.1 below). In the event that the working capital as determined in the Closing Financial Statements is greater or less than the estimated working capital, the Purchase Price shall be so adjusted between the parties at that time.

The final determination of the Purchase Price shall be made at such time as the accounts receivable of the Corporation as at the Completion Date are either collected or written off, as set out in Section 5.7 below.

Page **1** of **3**

Vendor's Initials   Purchaser's Initials

Any reference to a time or date in this Offer shall mean the time and date applicable in the province in which the Practice is located.

The Vendor and Purchaser acknowledge that the Brokerage represents the interests of the Vendor in this transaction, and is providing only customer service to the Purchaser. The Brokerage will deliver service with professionalism, honesty and integrity and provide known factual market information to the Purchaser to assist them with their own conclusions. The Purchaser further understands that the Brokerage also provides the same customer service to other purchasers related to such a transaction. Both Vendor and Purchaser understand that any information provided by the Brokerage is not legal, tax, or accounting advice, which should be obtained independently as required.

Whereas the Brokerage is serving under this Multiple Representation arrangement shall not be appointed or authorized to either the Purchaser or Vendor **for the purposes of giving and receiving notices.** In addition to any provision contained herein and in any Schedule hereto, this Offer, any counter, notice of acceptance, amendment or other notice to be given or received pursuant to this Offer or related Schedule(s), shall be deemed given and received when delivered to the assigned Solicitor as provided by the Purchaser and Vendor, by mail, transmitted electronically or to the facsimile number, respectively, in which case, the signature(s) of the party or parties shall be deemed to be the original.

The Vendor and Purchaser understand that the subject Corporation has been promoted in marketing material, including but not limited to content distributed by print, web and email. It is further understood that the Brokerage will continue circulation of such marketing material at least one (1) year following the Completion Date, but shall not include names of the Vendor or Purchaser, unless otherwise permitted in writing by either party.

The following schedules as attached are part of this Offer:

Schedule "A" ....Clauses and Conditions
Schedule "B" ....List of Included Assets
Schedule "C"... Excluded Assets
Schedule "D" ....Contracts
Schedule "E".. Financial Statements
Schedule "F" .... Premises Lease
Schedule "G" ....Staff
Schedule "H .... Associate Agreement

IRREVOCABILITY: This Offer shall be irrevocable by the .... until 4:59 p.m. on the .... day of ...., 20**15** (the "**Irrevocable Date**"), after which time, if not accepted, this Offer will become null and void and the Deposit shall be returned to the Purchaser in full without deduction.

COMPLETION DATE: This Offer shall be completed on the .... day of ...., 20**15** (the "**Completion Date**"), on which date the Purchased Shares shall be transferred to the Purchaser. Unless otherwise agreed to by both Parties, the Closing shall take place at the office of the Purchaser's Lawyer at 1:00 in the afternoon (the "**Time of Closing**"). The Vendor shall not book patients on the afternoon of the Completion Date, except where extenuating circumstances exist and both Parties mutually agree.

Time shall in all respects be of the essence hereof provided that the time for doing or completing any matter provided herein may be extended or abridged by an agreement in writing, signed by the Vendor and Purchaser, or notice delivered by their respective Solicitors why are specifically authorized in that regard and whom are assisting with the closing of this Transaction.

Page **2** of **3**

Vendor's Initials   Purchaser's Initials

Upon execution by both Vendor and Purchaser, this Offer constitutes a binding contract of Purchase and Sale, subject to the terms and conditions hereof. In the event of failure on the part of the Purchaser to carry out the terms hereof after all conditions have been satisfied, notwithstanding any other remedies available to the Vendor in law for such default, the Deposit held in trust by the Brokerage, will be retained by the Vendor as liquidated damages and not as a penalty.

Dated at .... this .... day of ...., 20.................

SIGNED, SEALED AND DELIVERED
in the presence of:

IN WITNESS
whereof I have hereunto set my hand and seal:

)
)
)
)

_____
(Witness)

_____
(Purchaser)

I, the Undersigned Vendor, agree to the above offer and certify that I have the authority to sell the shares of the named Corporation. I hereby irrevocably instruct my Solicitor to pay directly to the Brokerage, with whom I have agreed to pay a transaction fee, the unpaid balance of the commission together with applicable taxes, from the proceeds of the sale, prior to any payment delivered to the Undersigned Vendor on completion, as advised by the Brokerage to my Solicitor. I further allow my Solicitor to forward to the Brokerage, any further documents that will form part of this Offer as soon as it would be available and no later than fifteen (15) days following the Completion Date noted herein.

Dated at .... this .... day of ...., 20.................

SIGNED, SEALED AND DELIVERED
in the presence of:

IN WITNESS
whereof I have hereunto set my hand and seal:

)
)
)
)

_____
(Witness)

_____
(Vendor)

CONFIRMATION OF ACCEPTANCE: Notwithstanding anything contained herein to the contrary, I confirm this Offer with all changes both typed and written was finally accepted by all parties at ....

this .... day of....................................., 20.......... ....
(Signature of Vendor or Purchaser Executing Confirmation)

ACKNOWLEDGEMENT AND NOTICES

I acknowledge receipt of my signed copy of this accepted Offer as will be provided to my appointed Solicitor:

I acknowledge receipt of my signed copy of this accepted Offer as will be provided to my appointed Solicitor:

_____ Date _____
(Vendor)

_____ Date _____
(Purchaser)

Vendor's Lawyer:

Purchaser's Lawyer:

_____

_____

Tel: _____

Tel: _____

Email: _____

Email: _____

Page **3** of **3**

SCHEDULE "A" – CLAUSES AND CONDITIONS
FOR THE OFFER TO PURCHASE SHARES
MADE AND ENTERED INTO ON THE _____ DAY OF _____, 20 _____
BETWEEN DR. _____ AND DR. _____

SECTION I - SPECIFIC CONDITIONS

1.1 FINANCING/FUNDS

This Offer is conditional upon the Purchaser, at the Purchaser's own expense, obtaining financing for an amount up to the Purchase Price upon such terms and conditions as the Purchaser, acting reasonably, shall determine. Unless the Vendor (or the Brokerage or the Vendor's Solicitor) is notified in writing by the Purchaser or the Purchaser's Solicitor **within and no later than the** _____ **(_____) calendar day following the Acceptance of this Offer** that the Purchaser chooses to waive this condition or that this condition is fulfilled, this Offer shall be deemed null and void and the Deposit paid to the Brokerage shall be returned to the Purchaser in full without interest or deduction.

1.2 PREMISES LEASE

This Offer is conditional upon the lease of the Premises being successfully assigned to the Purchaser given that both the Vendor and Purchaser are satisfied with the terms set out by the Landlord for the assignment of the Premise lease. Both Vendor and Purchaser shall have the right to reasonably negotiate satisfactory terms with the Landlord, however, should either Party be unable to reach satisfactory terms for the assignment, this Offer may be terminated through written notice to the other respective Party and/or their appointed Solicitor, delivered in accordance with the provisions for delivery of notices in this Offer or any other Schedule and/or Amendment thereto, no later than 4:59 p.m. on the _____ day of _____, 20_____, and this Offer shall be null and void and the Deposit shall be returned to the Purchaser in full without deduction. If **no** such notice is received by either Vendor/Vendor's Solicitor or Purchaser/Purchaser's Solicitor respectively within the above time limit, then this condition shall be deemed fulfilled or waived, and this Offer shall remain valid and binding.

1.3 DUE DILIGENCE

This Offer is conditional upon the Purchaser and/or the Purchaser's Accountant, at the Purchaser's own expense, completing due diligence concerning the Practice Assets, the Corporation and the Practice. The Vendor shall provide reasonable access to the books and records of the Corporation and the Practice for this purpose. Unless the Vendor (or the Brokerage or the Vendor's Solicitor) is notified in writing by the Purchaser or the Purchaser's Solicitor **within and no later than the** _____ **(_____) calendar day following the Acceptance of this Offer** that the Purchaser chooses to waive this condition or that this condition is fulfilled, this Offer shall be deemed null and void and the Deposit paid to the Brokerage shall be returned to the Purchaser in full without interest or deduction.

1.4 LAWYER REVIEW

This Offer is conditional upon the Purchaser and the Vendor, at their own expense, having this Offer, its Schedule(s) and/or any Amendment(s) reviewed by their own solicitors, and being satisfied in their own sole and absolute discretion. If such findings are not satisfactory to either party and/or their Solicitors, an amendment may be requested, in writing, delivered to the other party. Should such requested

Page **1** of **14**

Vendor's Initials   Purchaser's Initials

revision(s) be unacceptable to the receiving party, the party requesting such revision(s) may terminate this Offer through written notice, delivered to the other in accordance with the provisions for delivery of notices in this Offer or any other Schedule and/or Amendment thereto. This condition must be completed **within and no later than the** _____ (_____) **calendar day following the Acceptance of this Offer** otherwise this Offer shall be deemed null and void and the Deposit shall be returned to the Purchaser in full without deduction.

1.5 ASSOCIATE AGREEMENT

It is a condition of this Offer that the Vendor agrees to be retained as an Associate of the Purchaser up to _____ (_____) day(s) per week, for a period of _____ (_____) months following the date of closing. Compensation will be based on _____ percent (_____ %) of gross billings collected less applicable laboratory expenses. Hours and days of associateship will be determined by mutual consent between the Vendor and the Purchaser. The Vendor and Purchaser agree to enter into an Associate Agreement with such Agreement being able to be extended with the agreement of both parties. The Purchaser may terminate this Offer through written notice delivered to the Vendor and/or the Vendor's Solicitor in accordance with any other provisions for the delivery of notice in this Offer or any other Schedule and/or Amendment thereto, no later than 4:59 p.m. on the _____ day of _____, 20_____, if an agreement **cannot** be reached by the Vendor and the Purchaser, at the Purchaser's own expense. Upon receipt of the above notice, this Offer shall be null and void and the deposit shall be returned to the Purchaser in full without deduction. If no such notice is received by the Vendor and/or Vendor's Solicitor, within the above time limit, then this term of contract shall be deemed fulfilled or waived by the Purchaser and this Offer shall remain valid and binding.

SECTION II
VENDOR'S REPRESENTATIONS AND WARRANTIES

2.1 The Vendor hereby represents and warrants to the Purchaser as follows and hereby acknowledges and confirms that the Purchaser is relying on such representations and warranties in connection with the purchase by the Purchaser of the Purchased Shares:

General Corporate

(a) The authorized capital of the Corporation consists of an unlimited number of common shares, of which the only issued and outstanding shares in the capital of the Corporation are the Purchased Shares, which shares shall have been validly issued and are outstanding as fully paid and non-assessable shares;

(b) The Corporation was duly and validly incorporated and is currently in good standing under the laws of the Province of Ontario;

(c) The Corporation has all of the necessary corporate power, authority and capacity to own the Practice Assets and to carry on the Practice as presently owned and carried on and the Corporation has all such licences, registrations, qualifications and certificates of authorization as may be required pursuant to the *Business Corporations Act* (Ontario), its regulations relating to health profession corporations or as may be required by The Royal College of Dental Surgeons of Ontario;

Page **2** of **14**

Vendor's Initials   Purchaser's Initials

(d) The minute book of the Corporation contains an accurate and complete copy of the Articles of Incorporation of the Corporation and there are no applications or filings which would alter in any way the constating documents or corporate status of the Corporation. No shareholders' agreements, resolutions or by-laws shall have been passed, enacted, consented to or adopted by the directors or shareholders of the Corporation, except for those contained in the said minute book. The corporate records of the Corporation have been maintained in accordance with all applicable statutory requirements and shall be complete and accurate;

Purchased Shares

(e) The Vendor is the owner of the Purchased Shares and with good and marketable title thereto, free of any claim, lien, security interest or encumbrances of any nature or kind, and as such has the exclusive right and full power to sell, transfer and assign the Purchased Shares to the Purchaser free of any claim, lien, security interest or encumbrance of any nature or kind;

(f) No person, firm or corporation shall have any agreement or option or any right capable of becoming an agreement for the purchase, subscription, or issuance of any of the unissued shares in the capital of the Corporation;

Vendor Status

(g) This Offer constitutes a valid and binding obligation of the Vendor, enforceable in accordance with its terms;

(h) The Vendor has never made an assignment in bankruptcy or been declared insolvent or a bankrupt by a court of competent jurisdiction;

(i) The Vendor has never been found guilty of professional misconduct by the Royal College of Dental Surgeons of Ontario, and there are no charges, allegations or investigations concerning professional misconduct pending or threatened against the Vendor or the Corporation;

(j) The Vendor is not a non-resident of Canada within the meaning of the *Income Tax Act* (Canada);

Financial

(k) All material financial and other transactions of the Practice while carried on in the name of the Vendor or the Corporation have been properly recorded in the books and records of the Practice;

(l) The financial statements for the Corporation for the years ended _____, 2014, 2013, and 2012 (the **"Financial Statements"**) (copies of which are attached hereto as Schedule "E") contain true and accurate information, reflect a true and accurate statement of the financial position of the Practice as to the date(s) thereof, and, where applicable, are in accordance with the books and records of the Vendor or the Corporation, as the case may be;

(m) (i) For the purposes hereof, **"Taxes"** means all taxes and related governmental charges (including assessments, charges, duties, rates, fees, imposts, levies or other governmental charges and interest, penalties or additions associated therewith) including Canadian federal, provincial, municipal and other income, withholding, payroll,

Vendor's Initials   Purchaser's Initials

employer health, transfer, sales, use, excise and value added taxes and all other taxes of any kind for which the Corporation may have any liability, whether disputed or not and all Canada Pension Plan contributions and employment insurance contributions.

(ii) All reports, returns and other documents filed and required to be filed by the Vendor and the Corporation in respect of applicable taxes or in respect of or pursuant to any federal, provincial, municipal or other taxing statute required by law to be filed by the Corporation (the **"Tax Returns"**) have been filed on time and with all appropriate governmental agencies for all fiscal periods ending before the date of this Offer, as first written above. Each Tax Return was correct and complete in all material respects.

(iii) The Corporation has paid all Taxes due and payable as reflected on its Tax Returns and has paid all assessments and re-assessments it has received in respect of Taxes. The Corporation has paid in full all Taxes accruing due on or before the date hereof which are not reflected in its Tax Returns or will have made adequate provision in its Financial Statements for the payment of such Taxes. The provisions for Taxes reflected in its Financial Statements (as delivered to the Purchaser) are sufficient to cover all liabilities for Taxes that have been assessed against the Corporation whether or not disputed, or that are accruing due in respect to the Business, its operations and property during the periods covered by the Financial Statements. The Corporation is not liable for any Taxes as the date hereof or for the payment of any installment in respect of Taxes due in respect of its taxation year end, and except as aforesaid, no such Taxes are required to be provided for.

(iv) There are no re-assessments of Taxes that have been issued and are outstanding against the Corporation. No Governmental Agency has challenged, disputed or questioned the Corporation in respect of Taxes or of any Tax Returns. The Corporation is not negotiating any draft assessment or re-assessment with any Governmental Agency. The Vendor is not aware of any contingent liabilities of the Company for Taxes or any grounds for an assessment or re-assessment including aggressive treatment of income, expenses, credits or other claims for deduction under any return, filing or report. The Vendor has not received any indication from any Government Agency that an assessment or re-assessment is proposed in respect of any Taxes, regardless of its merits. The Corporation has not executed or filed with any Governmental Agency any agreement extending the period for assessment, re-assessment or collection of any Taxes.

(v) The Corporation has withheld from each payment made to any of its present or former employees, its present or former officers and directors, and to all persons who are non-residents of Canada for the purposes of the *Income Tax Act* (Canada) all amounts required by law (including withholdings in respect of management fees), will continue to do so until the Completion Date and has remitted such withheld amounts within the prescribed periods to the appropriate Governmental Agency. The Corporation has remitted all Canada Pension Plan contributions, employment insurance premiums, employer health taxes and other Taxes payable by it in respect of its employees and has or will have remitted such amounts to the proper Governmental Agency within the time required by Applicable Law. The Corporation has charged, collected and remitted on a timely basis all Taxes as required by Applicable Law on any sale, supply or delivery whatsoever, made by the Corporation;

Page **4** of **14**

Vendor's Initials   Purchaser's Initials

(n) The Practice has no liabilities (whether accrued, absolute or otherwise) of any kind whatsoever except:

   (i)   liabilities disclosed or provided for in the Financial Statements; and

   (ii) liabilities incurred in the ordinary course of business since the date of the Financial Statements, which are consistent with past practice and are not, in the aggregate, material and adverse to the Practice.

(o) Since the end of the last completed fiscal year of the Practice:

   (i)   the Practice has been operated by the Vendor in the ordinary course and the Vendor has used his best efforts to preserve the Practice and the Practice Assets;

   (ii) there has not been any change in the condition of the Practice or the Practice Assets or results of the Practice, other than changes in the ordinary course of business, and such changes have not, either individually or in the aggregate, been materially adverse; and

   (iii) there has not been any termination, amendment or revocation of any license or any damage, destruction, loss or other event, development or condition of any character which has had or could reasonably be expected to have an adverse effect on any of the Corporation, the Practice or any Practice Assets or the future of the Corporation or the Practice.

(p) Since the end of the last completed fiscal year of the Corporation, the Vendor has not, in respect of the Practice:

   (i)   made any material change with respect to any method of management, operation or accounting practices or policies in respect of the Practice;

   (ii) waived or omitted to take any action in respect of any rights of substantial value or entered into any commitment or transaction where such loss of rights, commitment or transaction is or would be material in relation to the Practice Assets or the Practice;

   (iii) except as disclosed herein, increased the compensation paid or payable to the staff of the Practice or increased the benefits to which they are entitled as set out in Schedule "G";

   (iv) created any encumbrance on any of the Assets or suffered or permitted any such encumbrance that has arisen on the Assets since that date to remain;

   (v)   modified, amended or terminated any contract, agreement or arrangement to which they are or were a party, or waived or released any right which he has or had, other than in the ordinary course of business;

   (vi) become aware of the passing of any law not generally known that might reasonably be expected to have a material adverse effect on the Practice or the Practice Assets or the future prospects of the Practice; or

   (vii) authorized or agreed or otherwise become committed to do any of the foregoing.

Vendor's Initials   Purchaser's Initials

(q)   The Corporation has never guaranteed or otherwise given security for or agreed to guarantee or give security for any liability, debt or obligation of any person, corporation or other legal entity;

Practice Matters

(r)   There is no litigation, arbitration or governmental proceeding or inquiry, in progress, pending or, to the best of the Vendor's knowledge, threatened, against or relating to the Vendor, the Corporation or the Practice which, if determined adversely to the Vendor, the Corporation or the Practice, might materially and adversely affect the Practice; and there is not presently outstanding against the Vendor or the Corporation any judgment, decree, injunction or order of any court, arbitrator or governmental department, commission, agency or instrumentality;

(s)   There are no known facts, circumstances or conditions that directly or indirectly relate to the Practice with respect to environmental, health or safety matters that have existed or now exist and have had or may have a material adverse impact on the Premises;

(t)   Each of the Vendor and the Corporation has always conducted the Practice in compliance with all applicable laws, rules and regulations and neither the Vendor nor the Corporation is in breach of any such laws, rules or regulations;

(u)   To the best of the Vendor's knowledge and belief, all dental procedures conducted at the Practice were in compliance with all applicable laws, rules and regulations and were not in breach of any such laws, rules or regulations;

(v)   The supplies of the Practice currently are, and the supplies acquired after the date of acceptance of this Offer by the parties hereto will be, of a quality and quantity reasonably necessary to conduct the Practice in the normal course;

(w)   To the best of the Vendor's knowledge and belief, all of the patient/client records and charts are accurate in all material respects;

(x)   Schedule "B" contains a complete list of the tangible Practice Assets; all assets and equipment included in the Practice Assets are in good working order and condition and are in a good state of repair and maintenance, subject to normal wear and tear only;

(y)   Except as disclosed in Schedule "B", the Corporation is the owner of the Practice Assets, free and clear of any liens, security interests or encumbrances whatsoever;

(z)   The Vendor or the Corporation currently holds all permits and approvals necessary for the use and operation of the radiology equipment used in connection with the Practice; the Vendor or the corporation has carried out all required x-ray inspections over the last three (3) years; there are no deficiencies noted in these reports which have not been fully rectified;

(aa)   All client/patient lists, files and records of the Practice are complete and accurate in all material respects, and comply fully with the Regulations under the *Dentistry Act* (Ontario) and all privacy legislation as such law(s) pertains to the acquisition and retention of personal data;

(bb)   Schedule "G" sets forth the positions, date of hiring, work hours, salaries and benefits of all current employees and independent contractors (the "**Staff**") of the Practice and such information is accurate. Neither the Vendor nor the Corporation has given any verbal or written

Vendor's Initials   Purchaser's Initials

promises or made any commitments to any of the Staff that would change the information contained in Schedule "G" and no employee or independent contractor is in breach of any express or implied terms of his or her respective employment or independent contractor agreement. Without limiting the generality of the foregoing, no inducements to accept employment with the Vendor or the Corporation were offered to any Staff which have the effect of increasing the notice of termination to which any such employee may be entitled;

(cc)   The Corporation has the Practice Assets insured against any loss or damage by insurable hazards or risks, and such insurance coverage shall be continued in full force and effect up to and including the Completion Date;

(dd)   There is a good, valid and subsisting Lease (a complete copy of which, including any amendments, is attached as Schedule "F") for the Premises with the Corporation as tenant; the Corporation is not in arrears, in default or in breach of any terms of the Lease; the leased premises and all fixtures, plumbing, heating, electrical, drainage, air-conditioning and cooling systems therein are in good working order and condition and are in a good state of repair and maintenance;

(ee)   Schedule "D" sets out a list of all material contracts, written or verbal, concerning the Practice (meaning that the contract has an aggregate value for the purchase or supply of goods or services in excess of $1,000) to which the Corporation is a party; except as disclosed in Schedule "D", neither the Vendor nor the Corporation is a party to any contract concerning the Practice with a person with whom either of them does not deal at arm's length (as that term is defined in the Income Tax Act (Canada), as amended from time to time); and

(ff)   None of the foregoing representations or warranties contains any untrue statement of fact or omits to state any fact necessary to make any such representation, warranty or statement not misleading to a prospective purchaser of the Purchased Shares seeking full information concerning the matters which are the subject of such representations and warranties.

2.2   Except as otherwise provided in this Offer, the representations and warranties contained in this Offer shall continue in full force and effect and shall survive the closing for a period of twelve (12) months following the Completion Date despite any investigations or due diligence conducted by the Purchaser. Notwithstanding the foregoing, the Vendor's representations concerning tax matters in paragraph 2.1(m) shall survive for the period during which the applicable taxing authority may assess or reassess the Corporation in respect of the particular matter plus six (6) months. In addition, the representations and warranties contained in paragraphs 2.1(e) and (f) shall survive the Completion Date without limitation.

SECTION III
COVENANTS OF THE VENDOR

3.1   The Vendor hereby covenants that, from and after the date hereof to the Completion Date, the Vendor will and/or will cause the Corporation to:

(a)   continue operating the Practice in the normal and customary manner, to continue booking clients/patients, both regular and new, to the best of his/its ability, and to use his/its best efforts to preserve the Practice, the Practice Assets and the clients/patients connected therewith;

Vendor's Initials   Purchaser's Initials

(b) permit the Purchaser and his/her accountants and other representatives to observe all operations of the Practice after hours (at mutually convenient times) to inspect the premises and equipment, and to review all information, books, accounts, records, and other data and information relating to the Practice and the accounts, records and other data and information relating to the Practice and the Practice Assets, including, without limitation, all of the patient lists, files and records of the Practice;

(c) introduce the Purchaser to the Staff at a mutually agreeable time after all of the conditions for the benefit of the Purchaser in Section 1 above have been waived;

(d) not hire or dismiss any Staff, or increase or decrease (or make any commitments to increase or decrease) their work hours, wages, bonuses and/or benefits without the Purchaser's prior written consent;

(e) furnish the Purchaser with all information concerning the affairs of the Practice as the Purchaser may reasonably request;

(f) do all things and cause all things to be done to ensure that all of the warranties and representations of the Vendor contained in this Offer remain true and correct as if such representations and warranties were continuously made throughout the period up to closing;

(g) not enter into, and not allow the Corporation to enter into any contacts, commitments or transactions pertaining to the Practice or to permit or suffer any mortgages, pledges, liens, security interests, trusts, charges, rights or claims of other persons, or any other encumbrance whatsoever, to attach to or affect the Purchased Shares, the Practice or the Practice Assets, unless otherwise herein provided, outside the ordinary course of business;

(h) obtain, if necessary, any consents required upon a change of control of the Corporation for the contracts set out Schedule "D" hereto or upon the assignment of rights and benefits under those contracts from the Vendor to the Corporation;

(i) not sell, agree to sell or otherwise dispose of any of the Practice Assets except in the ordinary course of business;

(j) not change or alter the physical contents or character of any of the inventory or supplies so as to result in a material adverse change in the total dollar valuation of the inventory and supplies, other than in the ordinary course of the Practice;

(k) not publish, disclose, deliver, release, reveal or otherwise make available to any person or third party the contents of the whole or any part of the client/patient records, save and except for disclosure or delivery required to be made to any authority or body lawfully entitled thereto;

(l) pay, satisfy and discharge all Practice obligations and liabilities of the Practice in the ordinary course of business;

(m) not incur, and not allow the Corporation to incur any indebtedness, obligations or liability or make any payment in respect thereof outside the ordinary course of business; and

(n) promptly advise the Purchaser in writing of any adverse change in the condition, financial or otherwise, of the Practice.

Page **8** of 14

Vendor's Initials   Purchaser's Initials

3.2 The Vendor hereby covenants that, at the Time of Closing, the Vendor will do or cause to be done the following:

(a) leave all client/patient charts, records and x-rays of the Practice at the Premises for the benefit of the Purchaser as of the Completion Date, together with any charts of new patients acquired from the date of acceptance of this Offer.

(b) provide a list of uncompleted work to the Purchaser on closing (if any), including a summary of all prepaid fees on closing, if any.

(c) provide the Purchaser with a list of accounts receivable due and owing to the Corporation, as of the Completion Date.

(d) furnish the Purchaser with a statutory declaration confirming that the representations and warranties of the Vendor contained in this Offer are true as at the Time of Closing, as though then made, and that the covenants of the Vendor to be complied with at or prior to the Time of Closing have been complied with; provided that the receipt of such evidence and the closing of the transaction contemplated herein shall not be a waiver of the representations, warranties and covenants of the Vendor which are contained in this Offer.

(e) provide evidence reasonably required in the opinion of the Purchaser's Solicitors to confirm that at the Time of Closing, the Practice Assets shall be owned by the Corporation free and clear of all liens, claims, charges, encumbrances and security interests whatsoever;

(f) cause all necessary steps and proceedings to be taken to permit the Purchased Shares to be duly transferred to the Purchaser;

(g) deliver certificates representing the Purchased Shares duly endorsed for transfer to the Purchaser and cause the Purchased Shares to be duly recorded in the name of the Purchaser;

(h) deliver an indemnification to the Purchaser, in a form satisfactory to the Purchaser's solicitor, in respect of any misrepresentation or breach of any warranty, agreement, covenant or obligation of the Vendor or the Corporation contained in this Offer or the schedules hereto;

(i) deliver to the Purchaser evidence satisfactory to the Purchaser's solicitors that all necessary corporate authorizations authorizing and approving the transactions contemplated herein have been obtained, including resolutions from the Corporation;

(j) provide the Purchaser with a statutory declaration confirming that the Vendor is not a "non-resident" of Canada within the meaning of the *Income Tax Act* (Canada);

(k) resign as the director and officer of the Corporation;

(l) deliver to the Purchaser the corporate seal, minute book and share certificates of the Corporation and all documents, records, books, instruments and contracts of or pertaining or relating to the Practice and the Practice Assets;

(m) deliver a full and final release in favour of the Corporation, save for the obligations of the Corporation herein;

Vendor's Initials   Purchaser's Initials

(n) comply with all reasonable requests to ensure that the existing telephone number(s) and internet site(s) of the Practice are retained by the Corporation. The Vendor covenants to pay all outstanding charges (if any) so as to permit the transfer of the foregoing to the Purchaser free and clear of any claims by the applicable carrier. The Vendor further agrees to allow the Purchaser to maintain the Vendor's name in the applicable telephone and internet directories with the existing number of the Practice for a period of one (1) year from the Completion Date, provided that the Purchaser shall pay any expenses incurred in respect of such telephone directory or internet advertisements for the period from and after the Completion Date;

(o) deliver to the Purchaser a non-competition covenant of all associates of the Practice in the same form as the terms referred to in Section 7.2 below.

SECTION IV
PURCHASER'S COVENANTS, REPRESENTATION AND WARRANTIES

4.1 PURCHASER INDEMNIFICATION

The Purchaser agrees to deliver to the Vendor, in reasonable form and condition satisfactory to the Vendor's solicitor, on or before the Completion Date, an indemnification to indemnify and save harmless the Vendor from and against all obligations, commitments, liabilities, claims and demands arising out of or in any way connected with the Practice that are incurred on or after the Completion Date, except as otherwise provided for herein.

4.2 RECORDS RETENTION

The Purchaser agrees to retain in good order all of the client/patient records for the Practice in accordance with all applicable laws and regulatory requirements. The Purchaser agrees to make such records available to the Vendor for bona fide purposes upon written request without cost.

4.3 PURCHASER'S STATUS

The Purchaser represents and warrants to the Vendor that he/she is currently a registered dentist in good standing within the Province of Ontario.

4.4 VENDOR'S NAME

With the exception of the letter of introduction to the patients, the telephone directories and the sign at the Premises referred to above, the Purchaser agrees not to use the Vendor's name on any signs, forms, stationary or notices after the Completion Date without the Vendor's written permission.

4.5 EXCLUDED ASSETS

The Purchaser acknowledges that the personal assets of the Vendor set out in Schedule "C" will not be owned by the Corporation on closing.

SECTION V
ADDITIONAL COVENANTS OF THE PARTIES

5.1 The Vendor and the Purchaser hereby covenant and agree that, until the Completion Date, they will not disclose the existence of this Offer and the transactions contemplated herein (except to their own

Page **10** of 14

Vendor's Initials   Purchaser's Initials

immediate family members, solicitors, accountants, bankers and other advisors) without the prior consent of the other of them. After closing, the terms of closing shall remain confidential, except as required for government reporting requirements or as otherwise agreed by the parties.

5.2   In the event that this transaction is not completed, all confidential information obtained by the Purchaser during the Purchaser's investigations shall be kept confidential and all confidential documents provided to the Purchaser in respect of the Practice shall be returned to the Vendor.

5.3   The Vendor agrees that the Purchaser may leave the existing signs with the Vendor's name on them in their present style and location for a period of up to one (1) year following the Completion Date (or the date the Vendor completes his/her association with the Purchaser, whichever is later).

5.4   On the Completion Date, the Vendor agrees to sign a mutually agreeable letter of introduction and announcement of acquisition to clients of the Practice, in such form as is acceptable to the Purchaser; the Purchaser may distribute such letter after closing at his/her own expense.

5.5   The Vendor and the Purchaser agree to execute any document or documents which may be reasonably required from time to time, to give better effect to the terms and intent of this Offer.

5.6   The Vendor acknowledges and agrees that the Practice Assets shall remain at the risk of the Vendor and/or the Corporation until the completion of the transaction of purchase and sale contemplated herein. In the event that all or a material part of the tangible Practice Assets are destroyed or damaged or expropriated or seized prior to the Completion Date, the Vendor shall immediately notify the Purchaser in writing and the Purchaser may elect to terminate this Offer upon written notice to the Vendor. If such an election is made, the Deposit, together with accrued interest, shall be immediately returned to the Purchaser without set-off or deduction. If there is no such termination, the parties shall close the transaction of purchase and sale contemplated hereby and the Purchaser shall accept the proceeds of insurance with respect to any such destroyed or damaged Practice Assets. In this regard, the Vendor agrees to maintain adequate insurance on the tangible Purchased Assets up to the Completion Date.

5.7   The Vendor agrees to provide the Purchaser with a list or copy of the accounts receivable due and owing to the Corporation as of the Time of Closing. After closing, if any pre-closing accounts receivable are received by the Practice, the Purchaser and/or the Corporation shall remit any monies received to the Vendor on a weekly basis. Monies paid by clients on account will be applied first to any amount owing prior to closing on that account. Any uncollected accounts receivable on the first anniversary of the Completion Date shall be written off by the Corporation. Any amounts collected by the Corporation and remitted to the Vendor as aforesaid shall be credited to the final calculation of the Purchase Price.

5.8   The Purchaser and the Vendor agree to share equally, the fee, if any, charged by the landlord or its lawyer in connection with the within transaction.

5.9   The parties agree that the Corporation at the Time of Closing shall not own the list of assets set out in Schedule "C", such assets being retained by the Vendor.

SECTION VI
CLOSING CONDITIONS

Vendor's Initials   Purchaser's Initials

6.1   The obligation of the Purchaser to complete the transaction contemplated by this Offer shall be subject to the satisfaction of, or compliance with, at or before the Time of Closing, of the following conditions precedent contained herein for the benefit of the Purchaser (each of which is hereby acknowledged to be inserted for the exclusive benefit of the Purchaser and may be waived by the Purchaser in whole or in part):

(a)   the representations and warranties of the Vendor made pursuant to this Offer shall have been true and correct in all material respects on the date hereof and shall be true and

correct in all material respects on the Completion Date with the same force and effect as if made at and as of the Completion Date and as though Completion Date was substituted for the date hereof or similar terms throughout such representations and warranties;

(b)   the covenants contained herein to be performed by the Vendor or by the Corporation   on   or prior to the Completion Date shall have been performed in all material respects and neither the Vendor nor the Corporation shall be in material breach of any agreement herein;

(c)   no action or proceeding shall be pending or threatened by any person to enjoin, restrict or prohibit any of the transactions contemplated by this Offer or the right of the Corporation to conduct the Practice after closing on substantially the same basis as previously carried on.

In the event that the Vendor is unable or unwilling to comply with the foregoing conditions precedent, the Purchaser shall be entitled to terminate this Offer by notice in writing to the Vendor and the Purchaser shall be released from all obligations under this Offer and the Deposit shall be returned to the Purchaser along with all interest accrued thereon.

6.2   The obligation of the Vendor to complete the transaction contemplated by this Offer shall be subject to the satisfaction of, or compliance with, at or before the Time of Closing, of the following conditions precedent contained herein for the benefit of the Vendor (each of which is hereby acknowledged to be inserted for the exclusive benefit of the Vendor and may be waived by the Vendor in whole or in part):

(a)   the representations and warranties of the Purchaser made pursuant to this Offer shall have been true and correct in all material respects on the date hereof and shall be true and correct in all material respects on the Completion Date with the same force and effect as if made at and as of the Completion Date and as though Completion Date was substituted for the date hereof or similar terms throughout such representations and warranties;

(b)   the covenants contained herein to be performed by the Purchaser on   or   prior   to   the Completion Date shall have been performed in all material respects and the Purchaser shall not be in material breach of any agreement herein;

(c)   no action or proceeding shall be pending or threatened by any person to enjoin, restrict or prohibit any of the transactions contemplated by this Offer or the right of the Corporation to conduct the Practice after closing on substantially the same basis as previously carried on.

In the event that the Purchaser is unable or unwilling to comply with the foregoing conditions precedent, the Vendor shall be entitled to terminate this Offer by notice in writing to the Purchaser and the Vendor shall be released from all obligations under this Offer and the Deposit shall be returned to the Purchaser along with all interest accrued thereon.

Vendor's Initials   Purchaser's Initials

SECTION VII
POST-CLOSING COVENANTS

7.1　The Vendor covenants and agrees that subsequent to the Completion Date, the Vendor will　cause to be prepared by the Vendor's accountants and delivered to the Purchaser within forty-five (45) days from the Completion Date an unaudited set of financial statements of the Corporation as of the Completion Date (the "Closing Financial Statements"). The Purchaser shall have fifteen (15) days from delivery of draft Closing Financial Statements to approve or reject same. If the Purchaser approves same, the Vendor will cause the Corporation to file its income tax returns for the fiscal year ending on the Completion Date in accordance with the Closing Financial Statements. All costs of preparing and filing such tax returns shall be borne and paid for by the Vendor. If the parties are unable to agree on the manner of preparation of the Closing Financial Statements, the issue(s) in dispute shall immediately be submitted to binding arbitration conducted in accordance with the *Arbitration Act, 1991* (Ontario). If such arbitration shall not be completed prior to the due date for the Corporation's tax return, the Vendor shall be entitled to file the tax return on behalf of the Corporation in the manner the Vendor shall determine. If the parties, through arbitration or otherwise, should later determine that the tax return was filed in error, the parties shall cause an amended tax return to be prepared and filed and the costs of such preparation and filing shall be borne and paid in such manner as the parties or the arbitrator shall determine.

Once the Closing Financial Statements are finalized, subject only to the collection or write-off of the accounts receivable of the Corporation as contemplated in Section 5.8, the Purchase Price shall be final as between the parties.

7.2　The Vendor hereby covenants and agrees that he/she shall not for a period of five (5) years following the later of the Completion Date and the date that the Vendor's associate relationship with the Purchaser and/or the Corporation shall terminate:

(a)　directly or indirectly, an any manner whatsoever, including, without limitation, either individually or in partnership or jointly, or in conjunction with any other person or persons as principal, agent, shareholder, associate, or in any other manner whatsoever, carry on or be engaged in or be concerned with or interested in the practice of dentistry anywhere within a radius of ten (10) kilometers of the Premises;

(b)　disclose or otherwise communicate or make available to any person, firm or corporation the name of any client/patient of the Practice or the contents of the whole or any part of his/her charts, records or x-rays (except as required by law);

(c)　directly or indirectly, contact, solicit, interfere with or endeavor to entice away from the Purchaser in any manner whatsoever for his own account or on behalf of any other person or persons, partnership or corporation which carries on a practice similar to or in competition with that of the Practice; or

(d)　directly or indirectly, contact, solicit, interfere with or endeavor to entice away from the Purchaser in any manner whatsoever, any employee or Staff member working in the Practice on or after the Completion Date.

SECTION VIII
GENERAL

8.1 JURISDICTION

This Offer shall be governed by and interpreted in accordance with the laws of Ontario and the federal laws of Canada applicable therein.

8.2 EXTENDED MEANINGS

In the Offer, words importing the singular include the plural and vice versa and words importing the masculine gender include all genders

8.3 HEADINGS

Section headings are not to be considered part of this Offer and are included solely for the convenience of reference and are not intended to be full or accurate descriptions of the contents hereof.

8.4 ENTIRE OFFER

This Offer, including the Schedules hereto, constitutes the entire Offer between the parties. There are not and shall not be any verbal statements, representations, warranties, undertakings or agreements between the parties. This Offer may not be amended or modified in any respect except as written instrument signed by both parties.

8.5 TIME OF THE ESSENCE

Time shall be of the essence of this Offer.

8.6 SUCCESSORS AND ASSIGNS

This Offer shall be binding upon the parties hereto and their respective heirs, executors, administrators, representatives, successors and permitted assigns. The Purchaser shall be entitled to assign all of the rights and obligations under this Offer to a corporation owned or controlled by the Purchaser provided that the Purchaser continues to be liable for all of the assignee's obligations herein.

8.7 EXECUTION

This Offer may be executed in any number of counterparts, and/or by facsimile or e-mail transmission of Adobe Acrobat files, each of which shall constitute an original and all of which, taken together, shall constitute one and the same instrument. Any party executing this Offer by facsimile or Adobe Acrobat file, shall, immediately following the request by any other party, provide an originally executed counterpart of this Offer provided, however, that any failure to so provide shall not constitute a breach of this Offer except to the extent that such electronic execution is not otherwise permitted under the Electronic Commerce Act, 2000 (Ontario).

Vendor's Initials   Purchaser's Initials

Appendix F: Buy Versus Set-Up Comparison

OPTION #1
Setting Up a Brand New Practice from Scratch
• This comparison will assume the dentist who sets up a new office will work full time in his/her new office.
• If he/she chooses to associate elsewhere, revenues in the first year may be lower.
• Rent is typically higher for new locations (storefront facilities) than for established practices renting in more traditional locations.
• Marketing expenses are generally much higher for a new practice.
• Wages in a new practice will be approximately $75,000–$100,000 per year.
    — $22 per hour for a full-time receptionist
    — $18 to $20 per hour for a part-time assistant
    — $40 per hour for a part-time hygienist
• Laboratory costs in a new practice are typically very low due to a lack of established trust. This leads to fewer crown and bridge treatments in the early years of a new practice.
• Miscellaneous costs in a new practice are low due to the new owner's tendency to conserve cash and avoid excessive spending.

Disadvantages
• Lenders have strict financing conditions since new practices are a high risk with no proven cash flow
• Long hours with no profit for one to two years
• Many non-billable hours in a new practice spent waiting for new patients
• Working evenings and weekends
• Dental supply costs in a brand new practice are very high in the first year due to the purchase of long-lasting items that are not considered consumables (single use)

OPTION #2
Buying an Established Practice
• Lenders grant long-term loans with fewer conditions on a practice with proven cash flow
• Less staff training is required
• More billable hours per week due to many pre-booked patients
• Nine-to-five hours
• Hygiene is independent and needs little attention

Disadvantages
• Less ability to mold staff into your "ideal" office
• Wages are often higher due to long-term staff
• An established office requires more repairs and maintenance

For further analysis or questions about "Buy vs Set-Up Comparison" please visit www.roicorp.com or contact robert@roicorp.com.

	Option 1		Option 2	
GROSS INCOME	**Set up NEW**		**BUY a Practice**	
Per Month	26,667		70,833	
Per Week (48/year)	6,667		17,708	
Per Day (225/year)	1,422		3,778	
Total Hours per Year (1,575)	203		540	

GROSS INCOME BY PRODUCER		%		%
Owner	240,000	75.0%	480,000	56.5%
Hygiene	80,000	25.0%	370,000	43.5%
TOTAL GROSS INCOME	320,000	100%	850,000	100%

EXPENSES				
Fixed				
Rent, Utilities & Business Taxes	66,000	20.6%	48,000	5.6%
Insurance - Office & Liability	3,150	1.0%	4,250	0.5%
Telephone, Marketing & Promotion	24,000	7.5%	6,000	0.7%
Dues & Licenses	2,350	0.7%	2,350	0.3%
Debt Service (see below)	90,216	28.2%	103,272	12.1%
Subtotal	185,716	58.0%	163,872	19.3%
Variable				
Staff Wages	72,000	22.5%	232,700	27.4%
Dental Supplies	32,400	10.1%	53,600	6.3%
Laboratory Fees	8,300	2.6%	51,900	6.1%
All Other (office, repairs, etc.)	23,200	7.3%	37,000	4.4%
Subtotal	135,900	42.5%	375,200	44.1%
TOTAL EXPENSES	321,616	100.5%	539,072	63.4%
NET CASH FLOW	(1,616)	-0.5%	310,928	36.6%

CALCULATION OF DEBT SERVICE

	Set-Up NEW	BUY a practice
Investment Amount	$550,000	$850,000
Term (10 years or less for new set-up loans)	10	10
Interest Rate (Prime + 1%)	4.0%	4.0%
Blended Monthly Payment	$ 7,518	$ 8,606
Total Annual Payments	$ 90,216	$ 103,272

Appendix G: The History of Brokerage:
Oral Health Journal 100th Anniversary Column
by Timothy A. Brown

As Roy Brown walks down the aisles showcasing the latest in dental equipment, supplies and technology at the 2011 ODA Annual Spring Meeting, a smile comes to his face. An old friend and colleague greets him and a warm welcome and handshake are exchanged. This is his 62nd ODA Convention and while he still meets many old acquaintances, he laments that there are not nearly as many as in earlier years.

When he started in the dental supply business 62 years ago, there was no resale market for dental practices and no need for brokers. When a dentist retired, his equipment ended up in a basement or dump as it was not saleable and his patients moved on to another dentist.

All this changed in the 1960s when the brokerage business was born. The change stimulated by the "baby boom" initially came in the form of partnerships and group practices in dentistry. While this development was short lived, it created a need for a qualified opinion of what dental assets were worth — either for dentists to start a group practice or to form a partnership. Roy saw this need and the first "brokering" came into to play.

Initially, Roy faced obstacles. He was not recognized as a professional in the same way lawyers, accountants and bankers were. His philosophy that there was value in the "goodwill" of a practice was not readily accepted. His opinion was underestimated and the "goodwill" aspect of selling a dental practice was deemed to be worth only $1.

When the ratio of dentists to patients increased, patient flow became a concern. Young dentists with bills and loans to pay and retiring dentists started to advertise to keep new patient flow steady. Roy recalls that *Oral Health Journal* was the preferred venue for dentists to advertise their practices for sale. The number of pages with ROI listings grew significantly, year after year. If there was a problem or question, Marg Whittaker, at *Oral Health*, was for years the person to talk to.

Roy chuckles as he recalls Marg calling and saying, tongue firmly in cheek, "It's that time of the month again, Roy — get those ads in!"

By the end of the 1970s practices with solid financials and a large patient base had become valuable commodities.

Roy fondly recalls when he and his wife, Joan, worked for 13 years out of their house in a fledgling but slowly prospering dental practice sales business. Soon his eldest daughter, Lanee, joined the company and they opened an office together. Over the following 15 years, they established the foundations of a successful company based on good business practices. The company became synonymous with the appraisal and sale of dental practices.

For the last 25 years, Roy's son, Timothy, after having bought the business, has taken ROI Corporation to new heights of success.

The company is truly a family owned and operated endeavour, with Tim's wife, Sandy, and Roy's grandsons, Robert and David, actively involved. Today in Canada, brokers are licensed by the province (with the exception of British Columbia). The Broker Act ensures that they are qualified in communications, real estate law and sound business fundamentals.

Roy maintains that success in his business is based on ensuring the confidentiality of the listing and representing the seller exclusively. Canadian Agency Law allows for no equivocation in this matter and Roy firmly agrees with the law. He points out that he has an obligation to the buyer to be honest and forthright.

Brokers have done much to make Canadian dentists financially secure when they must sell their practice because of illness or a desire to retire. Many practices today receive multiple offers and sell for well over a million dollars. Compare today's prices with that of the first known dental practice sale, by Roy Brown in 1974 — for $28,000!

Roy relates many of the changes he has witnessed, especially with regard to the new technologies and procedures. He is encouraged by the large percentage of female dentists that have graduated in recent years. He recommends that graduating dentists spend three to five years as an Associate in order to perfect their skills and learn practice management skills. Then he suggests they buy an existing practice and run their own show.

Back at the ASM, Roy stops, recognizes and then reacquaints with another old pal and more memories are shared. It is easy to see that Roy still relishes his long relationship with the ODA and *Oral Health Journal*.

REFERENCES

Christen, A.G., & Pronych, P.M. (1995). *Painless Parker: A dental renegade's fight to make advertising ethical.* Canada: American Academy of History of Dentistry.

Clapp, G.W. (1916). *Profitable practice.* New York: The Dentists' Supply Co.

Cloutier, E. (1947). *Dental supplies: Investigation into an allied combine in the manufacture & sale of dental supplies in Canada.* Canada: King's Printer & Controller of Stationery.

Dickerson, W.G. (1992). *The exceptional dental practice.* Reprinted 1996. Las Vegas: Las Vegas Institute.

Domer, L., & Berning, R. (1992). *Valuing a practice: A guide for dentists.* U.S.A.: American Dental Association.

Downie, J., McEwen, K., & MacInnis, W. (2004). *Dental law in Canada: A complete introduction to Canadian dental law.* Canada: Lexis Nexis Canada Inc.

Ehrlich, A. B., & Ehrlich, S.F. (1969). *Dental practice management: The teamwork approach.* U.S./Canada: W.B. Saunders Co.

House, R.K. (1970). *Dentistry in Ontario: A study for the committee on the healing arts.* Toronto: The Queen's Printer.

Howard, W.W. (1975). *Dental practice planning.* St Louis: The C.V. Mosby Company.

Jacobi, H.P. (1967). *A dentist's flight manual to success.* Revised 1974. Wisconsin: Project P. Inc.

Kilpatric, H.C. (1974). *Work simplification in dental practice: Applied time and motion studies.* Philadelphia: W.B. Saunders Co.

Layman, G.A., & Redmond, P. (1977). *As your practice grows: How to hire an associate, form a partnership, build a group.* Tulsa: Petroleum Publishing Co.

Philips, E.S. (2008). *Your guide to the perfect smile.* Toronto: ECW Press.

Robbins, D.M. (2008). *Tales from the trenches: What you ought to know about selling your business — 14 alternatives to selling out.* Canada: Robbinex Inc. http://www.robbinex.com.

Schulman, M.L. (2000). *Change your practice successfully.* Rome, New York: Canterbury Press.

ENVIRONMENTAL BENEFITS STATEMENT

ECW Press Ltd saved the following resources by printing the pages of this book on chlorine free paper made with 100% post-consumer waste.

TREES	WATER	ENERGY	SOLID WASTE	GREENHOUSE GASES
7	3,276	4	219	604
FULLY GROWN	GALLONS	MILLION BTUs	POUNDS	POUNDS

Environmental impact estimates were made using the Environmental Paper Network Paper Calculator 3.2. For more information visit www.papercalculator.org.